WALKS
THE CHIL'

Seventeen Country Rambles around
Buckinghamshire, Hertfordshire, Oxfordshire,
and their borders

WALKS IN
THE CHILTERNS

Seventeen Country Rambles around
Buckinghamshire, Hertfordshire, Oxfordshire,
and their borders

Liz Roberts

———————

With Historical Notes

COUNTRYSIDE BOOKS
NEWBURY, BERKSHIRE

First Published 1990
© Liz Roberts 1990

COUNTRYSIDE BOOKS
3 Catherine Road
Newbury, Berkshire

ISBN 1 85306 081 X

Cover Photograph of Turville taken by Andy Williams
Sketch maps by Bernard Roberts
Illustrations by Pip Challenger

Produced through MRM Associates Ltd., Reading
Typeset by Clifford-Cooper Ltd., Aldershot
Printed in England by J. W. Arrowsmith Ltd., Bristol

To Bernard and the two golden dogs, Rosie and Moo, who enjoyed sharing these walks with me.

Contents

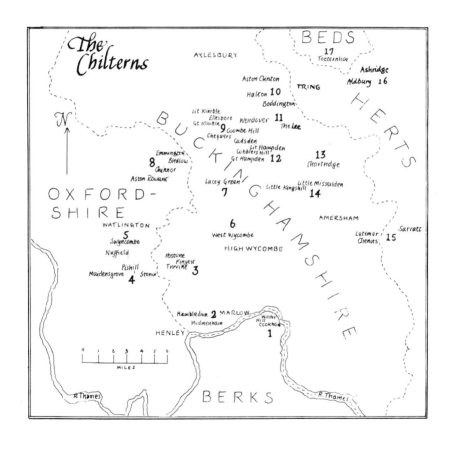

The Chilterns

BEDS

AYLESBURY

17
Totternhoe

Ashridge
Aldbury 16

Aston Clinton

TRING

Halton 10
Boddington

HERTS

Lit Kimble
Ellesboro
Gt Kimble 9 Wendover 11
Coombe Hill The Lee
Chequers

Cadsden

BUCKINGHAMSHIRE

Emmington
8 Bledlow
Chinnor

Lit Hampden
Wobblers Hill
Gt Hampden 12
13
Chartridge

Aston Rowant

Lacey Green
7
Little Kingshill
Little Missenden
14

OXFORD-
SHIRE

WATLINGTON
5
Swyncombe

6
West Wycombe

AMERSHAM

Latimer
Chenies 15

Sarratt

Nuffield
Postone
Fingest
Turville 3

HIGH WYCOMBE

Pishill
Maidensgrove 4 Stonor

Hambleden 2 MARLOW
Midmenham

Winter
Hill
Cookham

HENLEY
1

0 1 2 3 4 5 6
MILES

R.Thames

BERKS

R.Thames

Sketch Map showing locations of the walks

Introduction

Forming a gentle curve on either side of the river Thames some 25 to 40 miles from London, lie the Chiltern Hills. Mostly in Buckinghamshire, the hills stride south over the county boundary to leave a heavy footprint in South Oxfordshire, north-east to touch both Bedfordshire and Hertfordshire, and rise steeply from the banks of the dreamy Thames along its Berkshire side from Taplow to Mapledurham.

The hills are unusual in that the gentle, south-facing slopes are heavily wooded, the dense beechwoods spilling over the hilltops on to the steep scarp slopes to the north in many places. Not only beech but ash, oak, wild cherry, holly and whitebeam make up the varied woodland. Thorny scrub and bramble dot the barer slopes and, on the chalk, many orchids may be found, the commoner ones interspersed with the rarer pyramid, bee, spotted and fly orchids. Sparrow hawks and kestrels can often be seen hovering over hillsides while the cries of larks and peewits fill the air as they circle the cornfields below. Rabbits love the chalky downs and great colonies of them inhabit the Chilterns. Deer, the tiny muntjac and fallow deer, can often be seen in the cool woodland as fat squirrels hurry about their business in the autumn.

Furniture-making has been the chief industry of the Wycombe area and beeches from the surrounding woods were used for this. Bodgers, chair-leg makers, lived nomadic lives in sheds in the woods selecting and cutting the wood and fashioning chair legs with the aid of primitive treadle-operated lathes. These would then be sent to the Wycombe factories where the seats and backs were made. The original Windsor chair was the design of a Wycombe chair-maker. Many of the woods are very old indeed and some of the places are named after them; opposite Hampden House is Dirty Boys Farm and, near Little Kingshill, Little Boys Heath. Up-market Chesham retains the French spelling, Bois, but it is still pronounced Chesham Boys.

The Chilterns have been a popular walking area ever since the railway pushed out from Marylebone to Metroland, giving Londoners easy access to the countryside. There are 1,500 miles of footpaths in these hills, most of them well-used and well maintained yet, even on a sunny summer Sunday, one may walk for miles and see no one. The paths are often joined by narrow, twisting lanes, up and down hill, joining hamlets to villages to towns and yet the countryside remains unchanged and unchanging.

From the miles of footpaths I have walked, I have made up these 17 circular walks. I make no excuse for the fact that many of the walks start around the Wendover/Missenden/Amersham area as this is the very heart of the Chilterns. Every starting point has a place to park a car, but in some cases it is possible to take a real day off, leave the car behind and take the very pleasant 50-minute train journey from Marylebone to Wendover and I will indicate where this may be done and how to find the walk on foot from the railway station. Wherever possible, the names of good pubs and places serving tea on the route have been mentioned.

The short historical notes, given at the end of each walk, provide some information about the places visited on the walk and what to look out for. Stately homes to visit are thin on the ground but the walker will be travelling through old and lovely countryside, along ancient drovers' tracks and the even more ancient Ridgeway, and the Icknield Way, so old that there is no known root by which to place its name. It is a route trodden since at least 4,000 BC. Peaceful and undemanding, the hills will bring pleasure at all times.

The sketch map that accompanies each walk is designed to guide walkers to the starting point and give a simple yet accurate idea of the route to be taken. For those who like the benefit of detailed maps the relevant Ordnance Survey 1:50000 Pathfinder series will be useful. Please remember the Country Code and make sure gates are not left open or any farm animals disturbed.

No special equipment is needed to enjoy the countryside on foot, but do wear a stout pair of shoes and remember that at least one muddy patch is likely even on the sunniest day.

Many hours of enjoyment have gone into preparing these walks. I hope the reader will go out and enjoy them too.

Liz Roberts
April 1990

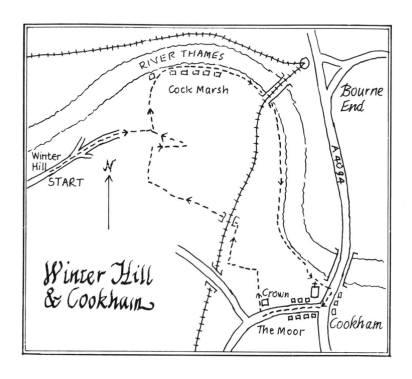

RIVER THAMES

Cock Marsh

Winter Hill

START

N

Winter Hill
& Cookham

Bourne
End

A 4094

Crown

The Moor

Cookham

Winter Hill
and Cookham

Introduction: This walk crosses the river Thames into Berkshire to afford sweeping views of the river valley and the wooded hills coming down almost to the water's edge. Downhill the walk proceeds along the riverside to the village of Cookham, over Cock Marsh and back up the steep slope of Winter Hill to follow its contours along the ridge.

Distance: 6 miles - an easy walk alongside the river but quite a steep pull up the hill later; well worth it for the views. Allow 2½-3 hours. OS Map Sheet 175 Reading and Windsor.

Refreshments: Cookham abounds with them: *The Bel and the Dragon* is of 17th century origin and charming, the *King's Head* opposite and the *Crown* on the moor all provide bar meals. *Bel and the Dragon* has an elegant dining room and an enviable reputation for the excellence of its food. The *Willow Bank* cafe and the *Two Roses* restaurant serve light lunches and teas and there is a Tandoori restaurant on the left just before the High Street opens out across the moor. The *Bounty*, on the river bank, seems to serve everything all the time. You pays your money and takes your choice!

How to get there: Leave Marlow over the magnificent suspension bridge, built in 1832, past *The Compleat Angler* towards Bisham, Maidenhead and Henley on the A404. Immediately after crossing the bridge turn left into a narrow unclassified road which passes under the motorway spur and winds its way uphill through Quarry Wood, where Toad and Mole and Ratty all lived in *Toad of Toad Hall*. At the T-junction turn left and continue along a narrow lane, bearing right at its end to park the car on the space available above the steep scarp slope of Winter Hill, overlooking a wide sweep of the Thames.

The Walk: Leave the car and proceed on down the lane along the slope of the hill, crossing the entrances to Stone House Lane and Gibraltar Lane on the left and passing a footpath sign on the right. On the left is a waymarked footpath opposite a beautiful old barn. Take this track and follow it downhill, ignoring side turnings, to Cock Marsh. Mallards, moorhens and lapwings breed in the marshy ground on the left while kestrels and sparrowhawks can often be seen on the hillside on the right.

As the path levels out it bears left toward the river. Follow the marked footpath ahead and then turn right at the next footpath sign behind some houses to the river bank. Carry on along the river path with Bourne End Marina on the opposite bank, through a gate past some pleasant-looking weekend/holiday bungalows and *The Bounty*. Soon you will see a large boathouse projecting from the opposite bank; Bud Flanagan, the comedian, lived in the yellow-painted house next door to it.

Follow the river path for about a mile or so, through some more gates to pass the clubhouse of the Cookham Rowing and Sailing Club. (If the delights of 'Olde Worlde' Cookham do not attract you, there is a good path cutting diagonally across the field 20 yards before the Rowing Club clubhouse is reached. This emerges on to the moor about halfway across. Turn right from it and walk to the car park.)

Carry on along the path beside a grassy area on the right. At the end of the grass turn right on to a gravel path through the churchyard where the artist Stanley Spencer, pushing an old pram containing his easel, canvas and paints, used often to be seen. Turn right opposite some pretty cottages at the far end of the churchyard and right again into the High Street, with the Stanley Spencer Gallery on the opposite corner. The gallery is open daily from 10am to 4pm and the cost of entry is minimal.

Walk up the High Street, with its many expensive boutiques peeping coyly from behind their pseudo-bottle-glass windows, and cross the moor at the far end in front of the *Crown* public house to the car park. At the opposite end of the car park take the path hidden in the right hand corner and follow it for about a mile, passing a footpath sign, and go under a railway bridge which carries the 'Marlow Donkey', plying between Marlow and Cookham. Cross a stile on the far side and, keeping to the path on the right and ignoring the one on the left, go on across the field with the hill rising steeply to the left and a small brake of trees on the right.

Immediately after crossing the next stile take a very narrow little path on the left which rises steeply uphill with a fence on the left. At the top, turn right and pause to absorb the panoramic view from Marlow in the west to Bourne End in the east. There are 3 tumuli in the field at the bottom of the hill; these are easy to discern from the hilltop. In front are the Hoveringham Gravel Pits, dug to provide gravel for the M40 nearby and now used as lakes for water sports.

Follow the grassy track along the contour of the hill for a mile or so and come gently downhill along the path to the right to meet the path on which you started. You may be lucky (or unlucky!) enough to see Concorde sweep overhead as you walk along the hill. Follow the track uphill again to the little lane, turn right and retrace your steps to the parked car.

Historical Notes

Cookham: This charming Thames-side village has been 'prettified' to extinction! It is impossible to buy anything practical here; butcher, baker and candlestick maker have all disappeared leaving only the boutiques, antiques and a shopping arcade where, if so minded, one could spend a fortune on articles totally unnecessary for ordinary living. This once bustling little village has become a 'gem' in aspic and the brasher, more modern Cookham Rise, on the far side of the moor has taken over the job of feeding and employing the local inhabitants.

Stanley Spencer was born in Cookham in 1891 and lived there most of his life. A plaque on the wall of the cottage in the High Street denotes his birthplace. Some of his best religious work was painted at his home between 1912 and 1915 and, in 1923, he painted the famous *Resurrection, Cookham* which hangs in the Tate Gallery. He was knighted in 1958 and died in 1959 at the age of 68. The little Stanley Spencer Gallery in Cookham houses many of his smaller works including wonderfully detailed paintings of the wildlife he observed so meticulously around him.

The nave of Holy Trinity church dates from the 12th century and the flint and chalk tower is of 15th century origin. On the wall of the nave, facing the door, is Stanley Spencer's *Last Supper*. The scene is the malthouse of the former Cookham brewery. Simon Aleyn, the infamous Vicar of Bray who held office through 4 reigns by changing his allegiance with each monarch, was also Vicar of Cookham in 1554.

Near the bridge is the cottage of Mr Robert Turk, the Queen's Swan Keeper. In July each year the ceremony of Swan Upping takes place, when all the swans are counted. The beaks of swans belonging to 2 City Guilds, the Dyers and the Vintners, are nicked - 1 nick for Dyers and 2 for Vintners. Unmarked swans belong to the Crown.

A sign on the wall of a cottage in High Street reads 'All fighting to be over by 10pm'; this refers to the cockfighting which used to take place in the village but was banned by law in 1849.

15

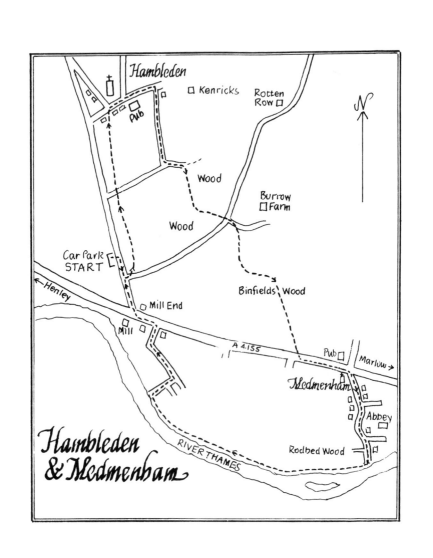

Hambleden

Kenricks

Rotten Row

N

Wood

Burrow Farm

Wood

Car Park START

Binfields Wood

← Henley

Mill End

Mill

A 4155

Pub

Marlow →

Medmenham

Abbey

Hambleden & Medmenham

RIVER THAMES

Rodbed Wood

Pub

Hambleden
and Medmenham

Introduction: This short walk goes through interesting and varied countryside, through ancient Chiltern beechwoods, pretty villages and along the towpath of the Thames. The Hamble valley affords the walker spectacular views and delightful glimpses of cottage gardens and grand manors. Along the river are water-loving plants such as yellow flag, marsh marigold and the Loddon lily. The walker may be fortunate enough to see a pair of herons which nest on the far bank near Culham Court. In the summer the scene is enlivened by the colourful boat traffic on the river. The site of the 18th century Hell-Fire Club can be seen in Medmenham.

Distance: A bare 6 miles - allow 3 hours fully to absorb the lovely scenery. This is not a walk to rush through and there are no very steep ups and downs. OS Map Sheet 175 Reading & Windsor.

Refreshments: There is a friendly village shop in Hambleden where additions to a picnic may be purchased and the pub, the *Stag and Huntsman* serves bar meals, as does the *Dog and Badger* on the main road at Medmenham. However there is nothing pleasanter, on a sunny day, than a peaceful picnic in the grassy meadows by the river.

How to get there: From Marlow take the A4155 toward Henley and follow it for about 5 miles. After 3½ miles there is a crossroads at Medmenham with the *Dog and Badger* on the right hand corner. Take the next turning on the right at Mill End (in about 1½ miles), signposted Hambleden. The car park lies on the left about ¼ mile up the road.

The Walk: Turn right out of the car park and then left along the lane toward Rotten Row. Take the footpath on the left toward Hambleden along the valley bottom beside the little river Hamble, which starts in the village of Skirmett and joins the Thames at Mill End. The pretty village of Hambleden comes into view ahead across the water meadows, enclosed in heavily-wooded hills which seem to stand guard over the village. In the autumn their brilliant reds and golds are breathtaking. Just below the fringe of woodland, high up on the right is Kenricks, a large house of red and grey brick built in 1724 on the site of the earlier manor house. It was the rectory of the much-loved Reverend Scawen Kenricks, who is buried in Hambleden churchyard.

Outside the general stores in the village stands the village pump on the green and, beyond it, the lovely lychgate of the church. The green is quite surrounded by charming old cottages of flint and brick.

At the church turn right and follow the lane past the *Stag and Huntsman* and a car park, both on the right, and on to a rough track. Turn right where the track divides to walk along the other side of the valley and passing Kenricks, the last house on the left, and the village cricket ground on the right.

After ½ mile turn left up the track and right over a stile 20 yards ahead. Cross the field toward a large wood, North Cot Wood, of mixed beech and conifer and notice how, on the right, the contours of the fields form concave and convex shapes and the beautiful patterns of the shadows the shapes make on them. Go over a stile uphill into the wood and walk straight ahead. Bear left at the top of the wood and then turn right downhill to a stile on to a lane.

Cross the lane, take the path straight ahead and then turn right after 100 yards to follow the wood's edge. Go over a stile at the end of the wood to walk between open fields. The timber-framed Burrow Farm house lies on the left beside some handsome cedar trees. Wild cherry, oak and hawthorn have been planted along the path and, as they mature, will give colour and substance to the view. There are extensive views to the right as Binfields Wood is approached. There is a splendid vista between the trees on the left, sweeping sharply down and then uphill, and on the right near the wood's edge is an old quarry pit from which chalk rock for building was extracted.

The path leads to the busy A4155 where turn left to walk along the road for about ¼ mile turning right opposite the *Dog & Badger*. There is a pedestrian path on the other side of the road which it is advisable to use. The church of St Peter lies in the trees on the left. There is a lovely mix here of old and new cottages and houses with some beautiful gardens. On the left at the end of the lane is Medmenham Abbey. The original Cistercian abbey ruins were the site for a Tudor mansion, which was bought by Sir Francis Dashwood in 1755. He added an arcaded cloister and a folly tower and used the house as a meeting-place for the intelligentsia of the period. It later became known as the Hell-Fire Club, with more sinister interests.

At the ferry point turn right to walk alongside the river. The small wet woodland on the right is called Rodbed Wood and is a Site of Special Scientific Interest, being the habitat of some rare wet-loving plants, among them the summer snowflake or Loddon lily, as it is locally named. Further along, on the opposite bank, is a square Georgian mansion, Culham Court, built in 1770.

Follow the towpath till you reach a house where the path turns right, leaving the river. Turn left into a narrow lane, another Ferry Lane, and turn left again at the main A4155. Walk with care along this busy road through Mill End past the cottages of Hambleden estate workers. Turn right as for Hambleden in the middle of the village and walk back along the lane to the car park. Hambleden Mill can be seen ahead through the trees as you walk down Ferry Lane. It lies on the left about 200 yards past the right turn into Hambleden. It and the weir are well worth a visit despite the rather desperate walk along the A4155.

Historical Notes

Hambleden St Mary's church, of 11th century origin, began life as a simple cruciform with a central tower until an east aisle was added in the 13th century. The tower collapsed in 1703 and a new one was built at the west end in 1721. This tower was embellished with 4 little turrets and encased in flint in 1883. In 1859 the 'sheepfold' for the local farm workers was converted into a south Lady Chapel; it would have been interesting to hear how the churchwardens of the time managed to get that one over on their parishioners!

The early 17th century gabled manor house was the birthplace of the 7th Earl of Cardigan, Commander of the Light Brigade at Balaclava.

The first Viscount Hambleden, the famous W.H. Smith, lived at Greenlands near Mill End.

Medmenham Abbey was built to house a Cistercian brotherhood founded in the 13th century. Only one pier of the original building survives. The present house is partly dated 1595 and was Gothicised when Sir Francis Dashwood purchased it in 1755. Architectural displays of their orgiastic goings-on were swept aside when a late Victorian stone Gothic south wing was built.

Culham Court is a Georgian mansion dated 1770 with terraced gardens running down to the river. George III visited the owner and was said to be greatly pleased to be served with hot rolls delivered by a relay of horses from his favourite London baker - in time for his breakfast.

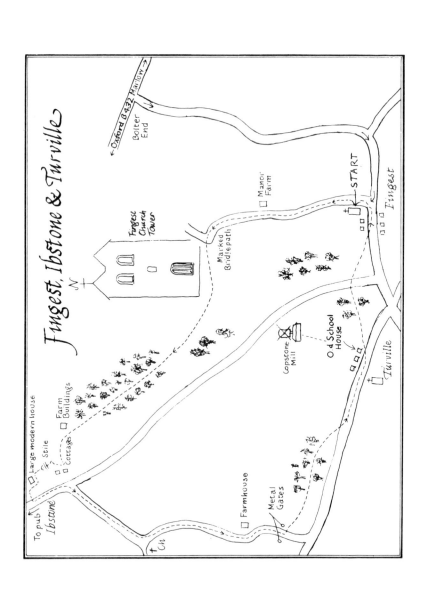

Fingest, Ibstone & Turville

Oxford B 432 Marlow →

Bolter End

Fingest Church Tower

Manor Farm

Marked Bridlepath

START

Fingest

Turville

Copstone Mill

Old School House

Turville

To pub

Ibstone

Large modern house

Stile

Cottages

Farm Buildings

Farmhouse

Metal Gates

Fingest, Ibstone and Turville

Introduction: This lovely walk, up and down the chalky ridges of the hills and beautiful at all times of the year, leads through 3 charming, unspoilt villages and through beechwoods and farmland. It has spectacular views over the Hambleden Valley as it sweeps down to the Thames and, just off the walk, is a 12-sided smock mill standing high on the hilltop.

The walk starts in the little hamlet of Fingest, a group of houses set around its Norman church, which sports a most unusual twin saddle-back roof to its tower, and meanders gently uphill through farm and woodland to Ibstone, astride one of the many narrow Chiltern ridges. It is here that the views are best. The walk then leads downhill to the village of Turville, a perfect picture of a model English village, though it is still a living, working community and has not been overly 'prettified'. From Turville a woodland path leads back to Fingest. There are a dozen or more variations to this lovely theme, but my suggestion is that you make this short walk and then, with the aid of the knowledge you have gained and the appropriate map, plan other walking treats for yourself in this area.

Distance: 5½ miles - a not too strenuous afternoon's walk. Some of the wooded tracks are used by horses and can be very muddy in the winter. OS Map Sheet 175 Reading & Windsor.

Refreshments: The *Chequers* at Fingest is renowned for its cuisine; even the bar meals are superb. The *Bull and Butcher* in Turville offers a good selection of bar meals. There is a pub at Ibstone but, on a sunny day, a picnic on the common opposite, overlooking the wooded Hambleden Valley, is a most pleasant way of passing the time.

How to get there: From Marlow, easily reached from London/High Wycombe from the M40, take the B482 for Stokenchurch. Continue on this road through Lane End to Bolter End and there, at a crossroads, turn left and follow the narrow, winding lane downhill for about 2 miles to reach Fingest. Turn right and park the car on the grassy verge alongside the church, with the church on the left.

The Walk: From the car follow the lane ahead, past some pretty, old houses, for ½ mile, passing Manor Farm and its old barns on the right. The road makes a very sharp right turn and here, branch off it to take the marked footpath/bridleway on the left, with the lovely trees of Hanger Wood high above on the right. Soon the path emerges into more open country with fields, topped by dense woodland, on the left and a narrow brake of scrubby wood on the right. Go through a gate into open fields with a hedge on the right. Where the hedge appears to part, keep to the right along the track with a wire fence on the right. There are views of open farmland and lovely undulating countryside, the hills tressed with beechwoods.

Go through another gate and shortly the path enters woods, the trees on both sides obscuring the view. The presence of dog's mercury indicates that the woods are of long standing as this plant takes many, many years to establish and colonise; its habitat is ancient woodland. Every so often, especially in late summer and autumn, the woods will rustle with the stir of pheasants picking among the dry leaves. Keep an eye on your four-legged friend if you have one! Through the mixed woodland, the path continues through a plantation of dark and rather gloomy conifers. Keep going along the same track, ignoring all side turnings, till a clearing with some farm buildings on the right is reached. Here turn left uphill on a broad track until a pair of houses and some barns are reached. By a gate the path bears off right across the grass and into the woods. Still progressing uphill, follow the path as it bears right and then almost immediately left to emerge from the wood over a stile into a field, with a rather grand modern house facing it. Skirt the house, leaving it and its garden on the right, and cross up the field to a stile in the far right corner. Cross the stile and turn right, then left alongside a gravel drive to emerge, in 10 yards, onto the lane at Ibstone.

If you wish to picnic on Ibstone's delightful common, you must here turn right and walk up the lane for about ⅓ mile to where the common lies on the left. The pub opposite serves bar meals from noon until 2pm. If refreshment is not required turn left down the lane with magnificent views of the valley you have just walked to the hills beyond. There are some pleasant brick and flint cottages and houses on the right. The appearance of the charming flint schoolhouse on the left is somewhat marred by an untidy-looking Portacabin as a sort of livid carbuncle on its end. At the village green, just past the school, the road divides, the lefthand lane leading down past Ibstone House to Fingest and the righthand one, a single-track lane, to Turville. Take the right fork here and, in about ¼ mile, the lane makes a sharp left turn and plunges off downhill. Ahead, 100 yards up a private road, lies the little Norman church of St Nicholas, which is well worth a visit even if it is impossible to get inside.

After a walk round the church, return to the sharp left bend, now on the right, and take the lovely little lane down into the valley in which Turville huddles. High hedges of dog rose, thorn, hazel and elder lead one to assume this to be a very old sunken lane. The grassy clumps in its middle might lead you also to assume that it is not now much used but don't be lulled into too much of a sense of false security; motorists do use it, especially at the weekends. In the autumn great trusses of scarlet bryony berries are intertwined with blackberry stalks and rose-hips, while the purple-red of the spindlewood leaves offsets the yellow of toadflax and blue of scabious in the hedge bottom. Walk past a farmhouse on the left to a woodland in the valley bottom, where the lane bears sharply left. Immediately after a pair of metal gates, one on each side of the lane, take the track on the left into the wood and follow it through the wood, walking parallel with the road and finally emerging onto it a short ½ mile from the village of Turville. Keep going on (left) down the lane, past an attractive conversion of an old flint barn on the left to provide a garage for the lovely flint 18th century house which comes next. There are more charming brick and flint cottages on the left and then a rather brash row of modern council houses. The little flint and brick church of St Mary lies on the right, surrounded by grim-looking larches and then, clustered round the minute village green, are a number of delightful timber-framed cottages and, just ahead, the *Bull and Butcher*. Next to the Old School House on the left and by a pillar box, is a marked path which you now take. Above, silhouetted against the skyline, is the 18th century Copstone Mill, an unusual 12-sided smock mill which, if you are energetic, you can walk up to see.

The route of the walk follows the path over the second stile on the right and on across the lower part of the field, walking gently uphill into woods on the far side. Cross the stile there and follow the path ahead, looking down to the right through the beech trees to the valley or uphill to the left where horses graze on the scrubby chalkland.

After a short ½ mile the path drops gently down to a stile into a lane. Cross to take the path opposite back to Fingest, turning right to go downhill where the path and road meet to form a T-junction. Go over the stile at the end and turn left to return to the church and the car. On the right, next door to the *Chequers*, is the pleasant 18th century home of Mrs Anne Laing who sells plants from an old farm handcart outside her gate. The bright colours of geranium and begonia, tagetes and marigold make a bold splash on a summer's day.

Historical Notes

Fingest: The tower of St Bartholomew's church is Norman - over 60 ft tall and with walls over 3 ft thick. The twin-gabled saddle-back roof is a later addition to this flint and stone structure with elaborate openings to its bell stage. North of the churchyard lies the site of the palace of the Bishopric of Lincoln. At the entrance to the drive of Fingest Manor is an old village pound for the collection of stray animals.

Ibstone's origins go back before the Norman Conquest; it is mentioned in the Domesday Book of 1086 when it was called 'Hibestanes'. The church of St Nicholas has many interesting features including a weather-boarded bell-tower, an exposed Perpendicular roof and one of the oldest pulpits in England. Copstone Mill dates from the 18th century and featured as the family home in the film, *Chitty-Chitty Bang-Bang*.

Turville: Though the present church of St Mary is of 13th-14th century date, a church was built on the site in AD 796 when the land was owned by the Benedictine abbey of St Albans. The first vicar, in 1220, was a monk named Elias. A continuous vigil of prayer takes place each year from dawn on 6th August (Hiroshima Day) to dusk on 9th August (Nagasaki Day) and the church is open from 4pm each day for prayers for peace and universal justice. A lunette in the nave has a delicate white hand holding a lily and was made by John Piper who lives nearby. In the north aisle is a memorial in marble to William Perry of Turville Park and his family.

Pishill, Maidensgrove and Stonor

Introduction: This lovely scenic walk encompasses a great variety of countryside; sweeping hills, wooded valleys and ancient settlements. It goes through the famous deer park of Stonor House which is open to the public most days in the summer.

The walk starts in Pishill, a tiny village tucked into a fold of the hills, and wanders up through the hamlets of Russell's Water and Maidensgrove. Now scattered with large, richly appointed houses, these little hamlets were settlements in pre-Roman times, probably because of their good water supply and ample cattle grazing. From Maidensgrove the walk leads downhill to Stonor and then uphill again through the deer park of Stonor House to South End. From South End the walk goes across fields and through country lanes to return to Pishill.

Distance: 8½ to 9 miles. There is some quite steep climbing from time to time so allow a good 4½ hours for the walk; time to stop and stare, too. OS Map Sheet 175 Reading & Windsor.

Refreshments: The *Beehive* is a free house at Russell's Water and has a restaurant, but bar meals are also served. The *Stonor Arms* at Stonor has an excellent restaurant, a pleasant garden and also serves good, plentiful bar meals. The *Beehive* is a bare ⅓ of the way along the walk but the *Stonor Arms* is just about halfway. There are beautiful places, such as Maidensgrove Common, to stop for a picnic in lovely scenery.

How to get there: From Watlington take the B480 towards Henley for about 4 miles to Pishill, passing the *Crown Inn* on the left. At a very sharp right bend with a house in front of you, park in a large lay-by on the left, just before the house.

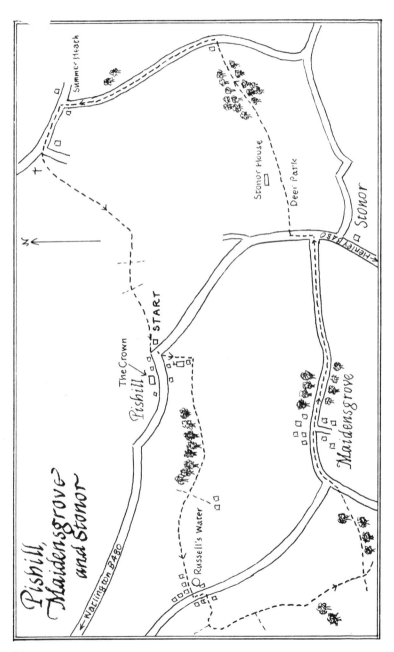

The Walk: Retrace the route for a few yards, then turn up a tiny lane on the left signposted 'Pishill Church' and with an Oxfordshire Way waymarker. The lane climbs quite steeply past the little church of flint and stone. Take the waymarked path at the top of the lane to avoid the driveway to the pleasant house of Chapel Wells and, ignoring the downhill path to the left, continue along the track.

The path now goes between high hedges of thorn, hazel and elder with Doyley Wood on the left and Pishill Bank on the right, where there are some quite outstanding views across the country. Go across a cross-track and straight ahead between farm buildings and straight on, bearing right past a modern house, across Russell's Water Common to the hamlet itself. On the left of the path is an old pond surrounded by bushes and many water-loving plants, among them yellow iris and kingcup. On the right is the *Beehive*, lying back from the lane.

Turn left round the pond and left onto a road and, after 200 yards, take a track on the right beside the Old Chapel. Turn right and then left to walk downhill with marvellous open views to the right. At a Y-junction bear left; there are steep grassy hills on both sides of the deep track. Follow the path through scrubby hedges ignoring all side turnings and across a crosspath alongside a small wood on the right. Walk on down the valley, the hills rising steeply on the left. At a T-junction take a path on the left through a gate, with trees on the right. DO NOT follow the track but head for a white stile into woodland across the field. Take care not to stumble into, or over, the dozens of rabbit-holes perforating the field's surface. The path climbs steeply uphill to the wood; pause at the top to look at the marvellous scenery over the treetops and fields.

Go over the stile into the wood, bearing right to wind up through the wood to another stile. Cross the stile and go straight across the next field to another stile into woodland again. This is a nature reserve managed by the Berks, Bucks and Oxon Naturalists Trust (BBONT). Take the path through the wood, cross a stile and then a field straight ahead to a stile in the left corner. Turn left over the stile onto a track and then right onto a lane at the top, coming out onto Maidensgrove Common. Follow the lane gently downhill to its junction with the B480.

The *Stonor Arms* lies about ¼ mile down the road to the right of the junction. If refreshment is not required, turn left here along the road for Stonor House and the deer park, among tall, straight-trunked beeches with clumps of dog violets between their claw-like roots. High, wooded hills lie ahead. Follow the road for 400 yards to a fence/kissing gate at the deer park sign. Enter the park by the gate and keep to the well-marked path as it climbs and circles the house in a bowl in the hills and with narrow deer tracks to left and right. Here you cannot miss the deer;

antlered stags standing majestically on the skyline, small herds grazing gently in the pasture, does and their young in timid stillness among the dappled trees. Note, too, the little flint chapel on the end of the red brick house. The path throughout is marked by white arrows surmounted by a charming spreadeagled frog.

Leave the park through an elaborate wire gate and follow the path through a conifer wood with rhododendron bushes along the way. This is Balham's Wood. Soon the path emerges onto a lane past a pair of cheerful flint cottages at South End. Turn left and walk along the lane, high above the landscape, for 1 mile to a T-junction. Turn left onto a busier road at Summer Heath and, at another T-junction, cross the road by a pretty house and take the path on the left as for Saviour's. Take the path on the left through a gate and cross the field to a stile. There are stupendous views all around; wooded hill upon hill into the far distance. Go across the field to a gate in the fence straight ahead and turn right onto a path.

Keeping the fence on the right, walk on over fields and stiles downhill through a small thicket. At the next stile go straight across the field and cross the farm track in the valley to continue straight ahead and slightly uphill. Notice the bowl-shape of the field on the left. Cross another track at the top of the field and continue with the hedge now on the left, over a stile at the bottom with a new plantation of trees on the right and a splendid creeper-covered house on the left. Cross the last stile of the day and turn left to a track leading back to the lay-by and the car on the road.

Historical Notes

Pishill: The little church at Pishill was rebuilt in 1854 to replace a Norman building. The south-west window was created in 1967 by John Piper who lives a few miles away at Fawley Bottom. The barn behind the rectory incorporates a 13th century blocked window.

Stonor Park is the seat of the Camoys family, the title of Baron Camoys having been created in 1383. The first Baron Camoys fought at Agincourt. Stonor Park has been in the possession of the Camoys family since the 12th century. The chapel of the Holy Trinity was built in the 14th century but was restored in 1800 and again in 1960. The Jesuit martyr, Edmund Campion, hid in the priest's hole in the chapel in 1580 and even set up a secret printing press there.

Watlington, Swyncombe and Nuffield

Introduction: This walk encompasses some of the most dramatic scenery along the Oxfordshire part of the ancient Ridgeway so that, all the way along, there are fine views of farmland, woodland, valleys and hills. The walk starts in the little market town of Watlington, tiny streets and pathways leading off the High Street to delightful 17th century houses.

The walk follows the Ridgeway to Swyncombe and then on to Nuffield and returns along the steep contours of hills overlooking the Thames valley above Wallingford. The final mile or two is a retracing of steps along the Ridgeway back to Watlington but the view is always different the other way round!

Distance: 11 miles - some quite steep climbing places so an all-day outing is recommended. OS Map Sheet 175 Reading & Windsor.

Refreshments: There is a pub, the *Crown*, at Nuffield halfway round the walk. It has a pleasant outdoor area in the front and serves bar meals and there are pubs and restaurants in Watlington, but easily the pleasantest way to have lunch is in picnic form on one of the lovely slopes looking over the valleys to the distant hills.

How to get there: As the B4009 from Chinnor enters Watlington it narrows to pass the old Corn Market, with the High Street off to the right and Couching Street ahead. Just as the road narrows, before the Corn Market, take a narrow left turn, Hill Road, and follow the road for ¾ mile to where the broad Ridgeway path crosses the road. It is signposted. There is ample parking space on the track on the left.

The Walk: Cross the road on to the Ridgeway track by the White Mark (see map) and follow the track for about ½ mile. On the left, through the trees, are glimpses of Watlington Hill, a grand eminence in the care of the National Trust, and Watlington Park built in 1755 and with some splendid specimen trees in its extensive grounds.

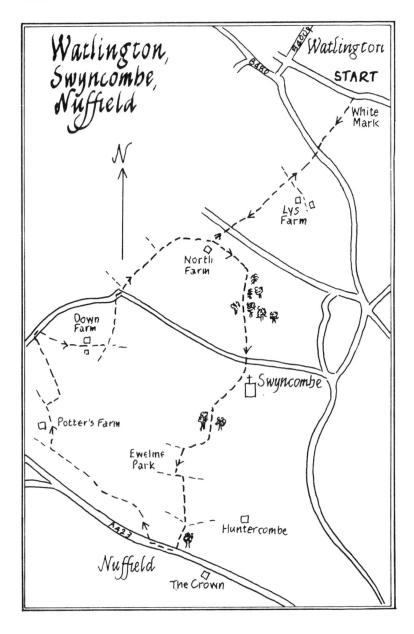

Watlington,
Swyncombe,
Nuffield

N

Watlington
START

White
Mark

Lys
Farm

North
Farm

Down
Farm

✝ Swyncombe

Potter's Farm

Ewelme
Park

Huntercombe

A423

Nuffield

The Crown

In another ½ mile the B480 is reached; cross the road to the lane on the far side and follow this to a junction of 5 ways. Keep straight on here passing 2 large, pleasant looking houses on the left and on to a path between straggly scrubby hedges. Cross the next road at the path's end on to the track opposite and follow this to a farm track on the left between a line of trees and a group of farm buildings. Follow the farm track uphill to the edge of a beech wood and, where the track divides again, take the right fork which skirts the lower edge of this ancient wood, bordered, in summer, by great masses of purple willow herb. Turn to look back the way you have come and notice Britwell House, set against a lovely hillside above Swyncombe Down.

Swyncombe Down is a Site of Special Scientific Interest and is particularly noted for its abundance of chalk-loving wild flowers; tiny harebells, sheep's bit (a small scabious), pimpernel and heart's ease pansy among them. The Orangetip butterfly and the Chalk Blue are frequently to be seen here.

Soon the path curves left and into the heart of the wood and then downhill to a path junction. Continue downhill alongside a large field where, in late summer and autumn, you will be almost tripping over the numerous pheasants and partridge feeding in the field and hedge-bottom. The path leads uphill to meet a little road. Go on across the road to the little 11th century church of St Botolph at Swyncombe, with some small and rather charming angel's faces on headstones in the churchyard. The Rectory and Swyncombe House, just round the corner, were built in 1840.

Leaving the church on the left, go through a gate and along a track curving right. After about ¼ mile take the stile on the left and climb uphill toward a wood. Go through the wood where, particularly in early autumn, you may be fortunate to see a variety of colourful fungi, especially the red and white spotted Fly Agaric and some huge frilly affairs sticking out around dead or dying tree-stumps. They are quite dramatic in this setting. The path emerges at the corner of a field. Continue on it ahead and as it curves right to a stile and a gate. Go over the stile and follow the farm track to Ewelme Park farm. Turn left between the farm buildings and on past the farmhouse, which has a beautiful garden and magnificent views all round.

After 300 yards the path forks at a pond and here take the left fork and, after another 50 yards, fork right and follow the path to a field edge. Go across the field to a white waymark post near the right hand end of the wood facing you. Go into the wood and turn left then, after 100 yards, turn right towards another large field and make for the white post nearly at the end of a square plantation of trees. Go through this, bearing slightly left, to the top lefthand corner of the plantation and go over or through a gate to emerge on to the road, A423, at Gangsdown Hill.

If you are in need of refreshment here turn left and walk a few yards down the road to find the *Crown* on your right. This is the hamlet of Nuffield which the famous philanthropist and car manufacturer, Sir William Morris, took as his title to become Lord Nuffield. Nearby is Huntercombe Place, a large Borstal for young offenders and, further on, Nuffield Place.

On leaving the *Crown*, return the way you came along the road, walking with care as this is a busy road, to a lay-by on the right about ¼ mile ahead. Turn half-right here on to a narrow lane and follow it downhill past 2 plain bungalows. Where the lane turns left leave it to take the path ahead between hedges and out into the open country. There is a dramatic view of the valley ahead with the road winding toward Wallingford and Didcot Power Station, a very modern reminder on a very ancient footpath. In the distance are Wittenham Tumps, a clump of trees on a high, bald hill.

Follow this path for about 1 mile to Potters Farm which lies below in a well-sheltered position. At the farm turn right on to the farm track and then right across the fields once past the farmhouse. Swyncombe Down rolls away ahead.

Turn right at an old cattle trough by the side of the path and follow the track for about 50 yards and then turn left into a narrow path running between rough hedges of thorn and scrub. At the T-junction turn right and follow a broad track alongside a field where large numbers of pigs are kept. They lumber inquisitively to the electric fence at one's passing but are mostly sensible enough not to touch it! The track runs downhill to a shallow valley and, at the valley foot, turn left along the other side of the pig farm. This is the Maternity Unit and dozens of pink piglets scuttle and squeal about the field. Follow this track for ½ mile to a road. Cross the road into a field and keep ahead with a wire fence on the left and then a hedge on the right to another road.

Turn right on to the road and, when it turns sharply right, follow the track straight ahead alongside another ancient beechwood on the left. Follow the track to the wood's end, where you should join a track coming in from the left. There are fine views all around here with Britwell House high up on the left against a backdrop of dark woodland.

Follow the same track for 1½ miles back to the 5-way junction at Lys Farm and make your way down the lane ahead, retracing the path taken earlier, crossing the B480 and then on another mile or so back to the car. Walking back there are fine views of Christmas Common and

Shirburn Hill directly ahead. Cross Hill Road to the car and return to Watlington. Hill Road is one-way at its end so a left turn must be taken and then a right turn into Couching Street to bring one to High Street and the Corn Market.

Historical Notes

The Church of the Holy Trinity at Nuffield is of Norman origin but there was a church on the site long before then. In the nave floor is a brass, dated 1360, to Benet English of English Farm and on the south doorway are 3 'scratch-dials', early forms of sundial used by the sexton to tell the times of the services. Two dials are upside down but the third is complete and correct.

Britwell House was built in 1728 for Sir Edward Simeon, who designed the small oval chapel on the south wing built in 1769. In the grounds is an obelisk with a pineapple finial. More recently the house was lived in by Mr David and Lady Pamela Hicks. Lady Pamela is the daughter of the late Lord Louis Mountbatten.

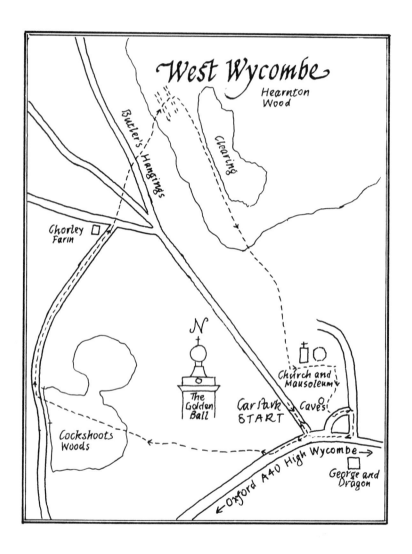

West Wycombe

Hearnton Wood

Clearing

Butler's Hangings

Chorley Farm

N

The Golden Ball

Church and Mausoleum

Car Park START

Caves

Cockshoots Woods

←Oxford A40 High Wycombe→

George and Dragon

West Wycombe

Introduction: This short walk traverses quite steep ups and downs through farmland, woodland and beautiful countryside, starting and finishing near the caves made famous by Sir Francis Dashwood and his friends in the 18th century with the Hell-Fire Club. The village of West Wycombe and West Wycombe Park are now in the care of the National Trust and it is possible, during the summer, to visit the house and its beautiful grounds.

Distance: About 3½ miles - about 2 hours allowing for rests and to look at the views from the steep climbs. OS Map Sheet 165 Aylesbury & Leighton Buzzard.

Refreshments: The *George & Dragon*, early 18th century, is worth a visit, not only for its ample bar meals, but also for its magnificent architecture, with a high arch into the courtyard where coaches from London used to stop en route to Oxford. There is a restaurant in the garden centre which provides light snacks and teas and the same can be had from the snack bar at the caves.

How to get there: Follow the A40 from High Wycombe towards Oxford, through West Wycombe High Street and take the right fork immediately after this, opposite the gates of West Wycombe Park, to the garden centre where there is free parking in a large and seldom crowded area.

The Walk: Leave the car park and turn right on to the road and then right again on to the A40 by the old pound. In the field on the right, called Long Meadow, is the source of the river Wye which runs through High Wycombe and provided a water supply for the industries of paper-making and furniture manufacture.

Soon take a stile on the right and cross a large field diagonally to a stile. On the right is a delightful view of the wooded hill on which West Wycombe church stands with its huge golden ball shining on the top. Cross the next stile and walk up the path through a cultivated field to Great Cockshoots Wood. Notice the predominance of flints on the surface of the soil; these stones usually overlay the chalky hilltops and help to retain moisture in the fields. They are, or were, widely used in local building because of their easy accessibility. Some new houses have been built with them in recent years. Little Cockshoots Wood lies to the right; on sunny days the long shadows formed by the trees on the undulating field surfaces are quite beautiful.

Keeping the hedge on the left, follow the waymarked path to a stile leading in to the wood, of beech and larch. Cross a track and follow the path straight ahead downhill to another track, a sunken lane believed to have existed since pre-Roman times. Turn right on to the track and follow it straight ahead, ignoring a left turn, and follow a grassy track now downhill and into open country. Here you may notice badger tracks emerging on either side of the track from the wood.

Soon the track emerges on to a lane by Chorley Farm. Cross this lane and 2 other tiny lanes, finger-like ridges running down to the valley at West Wycombe, by stiles and over fields. At the last stile walk uphill steeply along a narrow path keeping the hedge on the right and through scrub and woodland, called Butler's Hangings.

This is a nature reserve managed by the Berks, Bucks and Oxon Naturalists' Trust. The brilliant reds of the dog-wood branches contrast with the black berries of the buckthorn and the scarlet viburnum and hip berries, making a colourful display. In summer the hedge is decked with tall yellow mullein and ladies bedstraw and the hilltop abounds with wild orchids and dainty harebells. The rare Chiltern gentian may be found on this hillside.

At the top of the hill is Hearnton Wood but before entering the wood, pause to look back over the lovely countryside you have just walked, the field patterns and the various colours of the growing crops. In the autumn the rounded shapes of the bare, ploughed fields stand out against a backdrop of brilliantly coloured trees. Go through the gate on the right to enter the wood and follow the path more or less straight through, crossing 2 broad tracks. At the next track, turn right and on the left is a new plantation of beech with 'nurse' trees of Corsican pine.

Soon open country appears again and there are splendid views to the right - the landscape drops dramatically downhill. At the grassy car park area, bear right up a gravelled path to the church of St Lawrence and the mausoleum. Beyond this is a spectacular view of the dead straight A40 leading from West Wycombe into High Wycombe. Take a path to the left, leaving the mausoleum on the right, and follow it downhill to the caves. Go left down a lane and turn right into another, with some charming cottages on the right, and under a brick arch at the end of the lane into the High Street opposite the *George and Dragon*. Turn right and follow the High Street and the lane back to the garden centre.

Historical Notes

West Wycombe is dominated by the great hexagonal mausoleum and the church with its golden ball on the hilltop, 646 ft above sea level. In 1929 a large part of it was purchased by the Royal Society of Arts and the houses were repaired and modernised while still retaining their original character. The National Trust took over in 1934.

St Lawrence's Church: The church is medieval in origin and served the small settlements around its feet as well as the village of West Wycombe. It now has a Georgian nave provided, around 1765, by Sir Francis Dashwood, as were the stalls and lectern, in rosewood. The gilded ball on top of the church was added in 1763, a copy of one on the Customs Building in Venice. It is open to visitors from 2pm each weekday.

West Wycombe Park: The 18th century Italianate Palladian house, with temples and arches, a landscaped park and lake, church, caves and mausoleum are all part of a landscape scheme started with classic splendour by Sir Francis Dashwood and it is a debatable point whether he and his friends actually practised black magic in the caves, though they do have a somewhat sinister air about them. The mausoleum was erected by Sir Francis in 1762 with money left to him by Bubb Doddington, Lord Melcombe. The urns in the niches were to contain the hearts of members of the infamous Hell-Fire Club. Celebrated architects, Robert Adam and Nicholas Revett were employed to carry out the work on the estate. It is open in summer from 2pm-6pm.

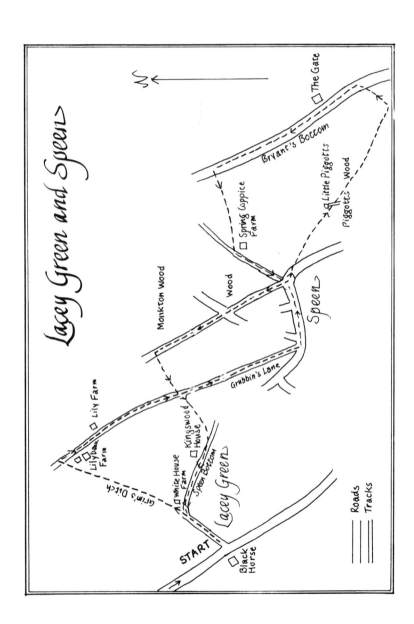

Lacey Green and Speen

The Gate

Bryant's Bottom

Spring Coppice Farm

Little Piggotts

Piggotts Wood

Monkton Wood

Wood

Speen

Grubbin's Lane

Lily Farm

Lilybank Farm

White House Farm

Kingswood House

Speen Bottom

Grim's Ditch

Lacey Green

START

Black Horse

Roads
Tracks

Lacey Green and Speen

Introduction: This pleasant walk starts on one of the many steep Chiltern ridges which dive down to converge in the valley at High Wycombe, and meanders over fields and through woodland, along ancient tracks and through the delightful village of Speen. It is beautiful at any time of year but especially so in the autumn and spring when the beeches are either unfurling buds of bright acid green, carpeted with bluebells around their feet, or dying to a burnished copper, when the patchwork of fields against them lies brown and ploughed for the winter or green with cereal and grass. Sheep and cattle graze lazily and the little muntjac deer and squirrels hurry through the woods.

Distance: 8 miles - not a very demanding walk though there are some short, steep ups and downs; a walk to take gently and enjoy. Allowing time to stand and stare you will need 3-4 hours to complete this walk. OS Map Sheet 165 Aylesbury & Leighton Buzzard.

Refreshments: The *Black Horse* at Lacey Green, at the start of the walk, offers a warm welcome in pleasant surroundings with good bar snacks. The *Gate* at Bryants Bottom, just about halfway, is a real old-fashioned pub except that a computer has replaced the old clanking till. Everybody who is anybody uses the Public Bar which has a magnificent log fire and scrubbed wooden tables. The food is good and there is a wide range of draught beers on offer.

How to get there: From Princes Risborough take the B4010 toward High Wycombe and after 1 mile turn left at a crossroads signposted 'Loosely Row and Lacey Green'. Follow this road for 1½ miles uphill and along the ridge through Lacey Green and, almost exactly opposite the *Black Horse* on the right, turn left into Kiln Lane and park on the wide grass verge.

The Walk: Walk on down Kiln Lane past some rather dreary houses on the right and some pleasant brick and flint ones on the left. There is a pond on the left and opposite this is a very happy barn conversion making a charming dwelling house.

Kiln Lane becomes a narrow track, Grim's Ditch, and there are splendid open views of the countryside as the track idles gently downhill. At a signposted fork in the track, turn left past the back of White House Farm and quite steeply uphill. This is a very old track bordered by gnarled oak trees and tall beeches. Through the trees on the left can be seen the recently renovated windmill silhouetted on the skyline at Lacey Green.

Follow the track for a good mile to a T-junction and here turn right on the broader way past Lilybank Farm on the right and, a little further on, Lily Farm on the left, an excellent example of the local flint and brick building. It is interesting to note that, hereabouts, flints are coming back into use in modern house-building. Their gentle light and dark greys blend comfortably into the surroundings to create a much less stark look to the new developments.

Carry straight on down this track, which can be muddy in parts after wet weather, for about 2 miles, ignoring all side turnings. Pleasant, isolated houses begin to appear after about 1½ miles and the last half mile is, more or less, metalled road with neat old, and new, cottages on the right. It is now called Grubbin's Lane. Before the houses rolling arable landscape is frilled by colourful woodland above it.

Emerge from Grubbin's Lane on to the main road through the village of Speen and turn left. Walk straight ahead through the village and downhill past small developments of new housing on the left and comfortable, older houses on the right, past Speen Baptist Church. Ignore the first track off to the left (Coleheath Bottom) and take the next lane off to the left, Spring Hill Lane, and go over the stile immediately on the right. Go on across the field and over another stile and walk diagonally across the next field to a metal gate. Go through the gate and along the track bearing left through woodland to a stile on the left alongside a metal gate into a paddock. Go on over the stile into the paddock at Little Piggotts. Cross the field to another stile and then go diagonally across the field to a small wooden gate in the fence. Go through this on a driveway and turn right, then cross the main drive to a footpath into Piggotts Wood. Walk straight ahead and steadily down hill through the wood. At the end of the wood cross a field and a stile into the lane at Bryants Bottom. Turn left and walk up the lane; a deep valley road with a smattering of comfortable houses and bordered, for the most part, by tree-edged fields.

About 100 yards from the stile is the *Gate* public house on the right. Walk on down the lane and about ¾ mile from the pub, take a marked public footpath on the left just by a 'Road Narrows' sign. The path leads uphill through the garden of a large house to a stile on the other side. Cross the stile and the field to a fence/stile on the other side and cross the next field to a stile in the hedge 100 yards to the right of a flint house. The stile emerges on to a narrow lane. Turn left and walk down the lane for a few yards and then take the marked path on the right into woods, opposite the gates of Spring Coppice Farm. Follow the path straight ahead downhill through the wood and turn right on to the track, Coleheath Bottom, at the end of the path opposite a house called Kingswood.

Follow the track ahead, crossing the minor road from Hampden Row and on to the same track opposite alongside Monkton Wood. After ½ mile take a left turn down a well-trodden path between metal fencing and hedge. Cross the track at the foot of the path and go straight ahead over a field into King's Wood, following the path steadily downhill to a broad, stony track, Speen Bottom, waymarked as a Public Bridleway. Here turn right and follow the track gently uphill. Kingswood House stands, stark and square, on the hillside on the right and the fields rise steeply up on either side of the sunken track. Walk past the side of White House Farm on the right and bear left uphill back into Kiln Lane and to the car.

Historical Notes

Lacey Green: In Kiln Lane an old house called Malmsmead once housed 2 notorious housebreakers, Smithson and Sikes. They appeared to be respectable gentlemen, travelling to London each day to their offices, but they were, in fact, carrying out burglaries throughout 17 counties, accruing thus property valued at a quarter of a million pounds. They and their stolen property were finally tracked down at Lacey Green and the 2 gentlemen spent a considerable time as guests of His Majesty, King George V.

Probably the oldest smock mill in England stands back from the road at the highest point in Lacey Green. Built in Chesham in 1650, and erected on its present site in 1821, it was a working mill till 1917. The restored mill is now open to the public on Sundays and Bank Holidays in the afternoons from 3pm to 6pm.

The *Pink and Lily* public house in Pink Road was a haunt of Rupert Brooke and his poet friends before the First World War.

Speen: From a mere handful of cottages in Domesday time, the village of Speen began to grow during the 17th and 18th centuries and there has been much growth since 1965, but most of the housing retains the old brick and flint style. One cottage, The Roses, was in the 1800s a lace school. Girls from the age of 3 would learn the craft of lace-making while the Dame who ran the school taught the three R's. There is still a great interest in bobbin lace-making in the village.

Bodgers lived and worked in rough sheds in the Hampden Woods producing chair-legs for the Wycombe furniture trade, working with a primitive treadle-operated lathe to turn the wood. Beech was especially favoured for legs and chair backs as it curves pliantly without breaking.

Since 1886 there has been a Rest Home for retired horses in Speen; little was heard of it until *Sefton*, the horse injured in the Hyde Park bombing, was retired there. The home is open to the public from 2pm to 4pm each day.

Piggotts, down Flower Bottom Lane, was the home and studio of Eric Gill, the type designer and sculptor who died during the Second World War. Though a Roman Catholic, Gill asked to be buried in the churchyard of the Baptist church at Speen. Before the war, many students of letter-form, among them David Kindersley, worked as assistants to Gill at Piggotts and learned their craft from the master. His home was a venue for artists, musicians and young intelligentsia of all sorts, and it is now a musical venue where concerts are performed during the summer months.

At Speen Bottom is the *Plough Inn*, run for many years by Ishbel MacDonald, daughter of Ramsay MacDonald and it was here that Gill and his friends and fellow artists would often congregate for a convivial evening.

Chinnor, Bledlow and Emmington

Introduction: This walk follows the course of the ancient Lower Icknield Way, the 'fine weather' route for trade and traffic in Ancient British times and, later, climbs gently to the Upper Icknield Way, the Ridgeway. Alongside the lower track, to the left, can be seen the wooded contours of the hills, while the broad fields of the Oxfordshire plain occupy the eye to the right. The walk traverses the villages of Aston Rowant, Bledlow, Henton and the tiny hamlet of Emmington before returning over the fields to Chinnor. The tall chimneys of Chinnor cement works provide a good landmark along the way. It is simple, as will be shown, to divide this 13-mile walk into 2 halves but, as the first three-quarters of it is on flat, even ground, the mileage is not as daunting as it may seem. Some parts of the route are more scenic than others but there is something to rest the eye and enjoy all the way.

Distance: 5 or 13 miles. The 5 mile walk will take 2 to 2½ hours but allow a good 5 hours for the whole route. OS Map Sheet 165 Aylesbury & Leighton Buzzard.

Refreshments: There are numerous pubs in Chinnor. *The Lions of Bledlow* offers a warm welcome and a very high standard of pub lunches as does the *Peacock* at Henton, just a few yards off the walk, further down the village on the right.

How to get there: From High Wycombe, which may be reached from the M40 out of London, take the A4010 (Aylesbury) road and, at Little Kimble, turn left by Kimble Motors onto the B4009, signposted to Longwick and Chinnor. Bear left under the railway bridge and follow the road across the roundabout at Longwick into Chinnor. After about 1 mile into the town, the B4009 turns left at a crossroads. Proceed straight across this crossroads into Mill Lane and park the car on the rough track about ½ mile ahead, just past the derestriction sign.

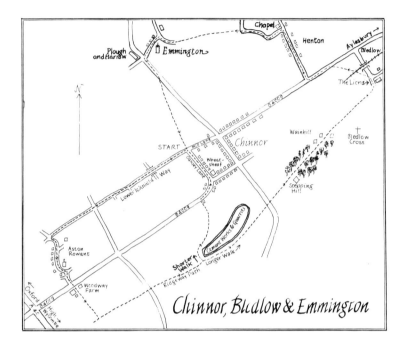

Chinnor, Bledlow & Emmington

The Walk: Follow the track ahead for about 2 miles, crossing a stream by a splendid concrete bridge, then a ford by a plank bridge, and a minor road. After the little road the track becomes more enclosed by tall, variegated hedges of thorn, elder, hazel and briar - a very old hedge indeed. The colours of leaves and berries in the autumn are spectacular and, in the summer, the scent from the profusion of blossom is quite heady. In the hedge bottoms are masses of marestail, a dull plant of uniform green and narrow, spiky leaves, whose claim to fame is that it is the oldest plant in Great Britain, perhaps in the world.

About ½ mile from the minor road, the path reaches a T-junction and here turn left along the track up to Aston Rowant. Ignore the farm track on the left after 100 yards and continue until the track becomes a metalled lane with some charming thatched cottages beside it on the right. To the left is a larger, Tudor, house with splendid traditional topiary of boxwood, the scent of which is pungent on a hot, sunny day. Fork right at the 13th century church of St Peter and St Paul to walk on past some extravagantly modern houses. Here the wooded hills are seen ahead and, looming above them, the Dalek-like structure of the Post Office tower on Kingston Hill.

At the top of the lane cross the B4009 with care and take the track past Woodway Farm. Follow this track to a narrow brake of trees where you turn left on to a broad ride, the Ridgeway. Alongside runs the course of a now disused railway which used to ply between Watlington and Princes Risborough and whose small tank engine was affectionately known by the locals as 'The Watlington Flier'. Cross a minor road after about ½ mile and continue on along the track. Notice how the upper slopes of the fields on the right tend to become almost white as they are frilled by the beechwoods. The chalkiness of the soil is more apparent higher up the hills.

If you are taking the SHORT CUT, at a T-junction, where the Ridgeway path begins to climb uphill, turn left and then right after 150 yards to skirt the cement workings. On a sunny day the water at the bottom of the chalky diggings appears blue-green against the cliff-like white quarry and the scene is reminiscent of some quiet inlet on one of the Balearic Islands. In summer the path here is gloriously colourful with dog roses and ragwort; in the autumn there are masses of luscious blackberries to quench the thirst.

After about ¼ mile turn left on to a path alongside a hedge straight down to the road. This is the busy B4009 again so turn right and cross the road to keep on a wide grass verge and then the footpath in to Chinnor. Bear left on the footpath into Oakley Lane; the *Wheatsheaf* pub is on the right hand corner. Go on down to the end of Oakley Lane where it meets the track on which the walk started. Turn right and find the car a few yards up the track.

TO CONTINUE, don't turn left at the T-junction but go on straight ahead, gradually climbing uphill along the Ridgeway for about 3 miles. Soon the track becomes a broad avenue bordered by high hedges and then, crossing a minor road, there are marvellous views of open country dropping away to the left and the wooded side of Wainhill to the right. Ignore the first track on the left and go on past a rather grand house on the right called 'Stepping Hill'. Keep to the marked (Ridgeway) path, ignoring side turnings, through thick mixed woodland of oak, ash, beech and hawthorn until a house can be seen directly ahead. At this house, Wainhill House, turn left and pause to absorb the view. Bledlow Cross is carved in the chalk to the right and ahead, in the far distance, lies Cymbeline's Mount with its distinctive clump of trees on its otherwise bald pate and the Coombe Hill Monument, set up to commemorate the fallen in the Boer War. Looking along the line of hills from Cymbeline's Mount, Whiteleaf Cross stands out, a livid scar in the wooded background; this is much easier to see than Bledlow Cross.

Walk on down the track ahead and after about ½ mile take a left fork, marked 'Footpath Only', to Bledlow, emerging on to the road outside *The Lions*. Turn left and walk down the lane from the pub and, in 100 yards, turn left again at a footpath sign across a field to a stile. Go over a railway line (the same disused one), across the cricket field to a stile opposite, over a ditch and across a cultivated field to a stile in the hedge. Bear a little left to a bridge/stile in the next, grass field and across the next grass field to a stile on to the road. Turn left and cross the road, then take the turning on the right, signposted to Henton village. In ¾ of a mile down the lane turn left on to another lane with a derelict tin chapel on the corner, opposite a rather bare red-brick bungalow standing all on its own. The lane deteriorates quickly into a track and, after making a sharp right angle turn off it, take the farm track on the left and follow it across the flat country to Emmington.

At the farm at the bottom of the track turn left into the village lane. After about 200 yards notice the sign for St Nicholas' church in the hedge in front of a rather rundown cottage. The tiny church is quite invisible within a thick clump of trees; its tower only can be seen on turning left at the lane end opposite the *Plough and Harrow*. After this left turn, carry on up the road for ¼ mile and then take the waymarked footpath on the righthand side of the road. Scramble through the hedge and go straight on across 3 fields, hugging the hedge on the right, to a very awkward stile on to the starting point of the walk - the Lower Icknield Way opposite your parked car.

Historical Notes

Cymbeline's Mount: This is thought to have been the stronghold of the British king, Cunobelin, from whom two local villages, Little and Great Kimble take their names. Relics indicate that there was a Romano-British village, a Roman villa and a Neolithic hillcamp in the vicinity.

Whiteleaf Cross: The cross, which lies on the scarp slope of the hills below the village, has a broad triangular base with arms nearly 7 metres wide. Like Bledlow Cross, its origins are obscure; it may have been a local boundary mark. Some say it is a pagan sign carved in the chalk and originally somewhat phallic in appearance, which, with the coming of Christianity, was transformed by the carving of the crosspiece to make a cuniform shape which robbed it of its pagan associations. You can believe which you like!

Coombe Hill, Cadsden and Kimble

Introduction: The walk starts in Wendover, a small market town set in a gap in the Chiltern scarp and framed in wooded hills. Though it now has many suburban estates, the 17th-18th century centre is still charming and unspoiled. Pound Street, which runs downhill to High Street, has some delightful brick and timber-framed cottages on the south side owned, until recently, by the lord of the manor, who also owned the cobbled area outside the modern supermarket, now used for the bi-annual fair and the Thursday market. This, with a grassy stretch dotted with lime trees in the Aylesbury Road, is known as Manor Waste.

From Wendover the walk turns uphill to reach the summit of Coombe Hill, the highest point in the Chiltern range, and across chalk downland and fields passing Chequers, the Prime Minister's country retreat, to Cadsden - 4 tiny houses and a pub!

From Cadsden the walk returns to Wendover through the hamlets of Askett, Butler's Cross and Kimble with the hills on the right and the lush farmland of the Vale of Aylesbury on the left.

Distance: 8½ miles - allow a good 3 hours for this truly magnificent walk. There is so much to delight; scenery, trees, wild flowers and buildings of interest that it would be a pity, indeed, to hurry the walk. There is some quite steep climbing for the first bit but the return walk is gentle apart from the proliferation of stiles to be crossed. OS Map Sheet 165 Aylesbury & Leighton Buzzard.

Refreshments: The *Plough* at Cadsden offers a welcome break in the middle of the walk. There is a pleasant grassy area with picnic tables outside and a warm welcome inside provided, as the courteous notice on the door requests, muddy boots are removed. This is the only pub actually on the Ridgeway in all its 80 mile length. The *Bernard Arms* at Great Kimble offers bar meals. At the junction of Pound Street and the A413 in Wendover there is a cafe on either corner and both serve light lunches, coffee and tea and, of course there are lots of pubs in Wendover, notably the *Red Lion* in the High Street.

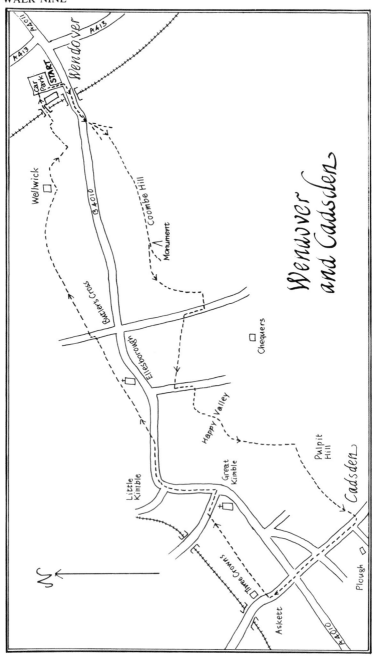

Wendover and Cadsden

How to get there: On the A413 Amersham to Aylesbury road, 11 miles from Amersham, enter Wendover along South Street, with its pretty cottages and some plain, small council houses on each side. At the roundabout, where the A413 turns right for Aylesbury, turn left to take the B4010, Pound Street, signposted to Ellesborough and after a short ¼ mile, turn right into Station Approach at the *Shoulder of Mutton* and go on to the Pay & Display car park just past the station building. Park the car here.

If you would like a real day off, leaving the car behind, it is very simple to take the train which runs hourly from Marylebone and, after Harrow, there are lovely views of the Chilterns to admire on your journey. The walk starts and ends at the station.

The Walk: Return up Station Approach and where it meets the B4010 turn right and walk uphill for about ¼ mile until an open lay-by and a broad track can be seen on the left, on a sharp righthand bend of the road. Cross the road with caution and take to the track and, just beyond a wooden fence with a 'No Horses' sign on it, take the middle path uphill by means of shallow steps. Very soon, on the left, the path divides, one bit going up steep, rather awkward steps cut in the chalk and the other, lower, path winding more gently uphill. Take either route as they both arrive soon at an open grassy space about halfway up the hill. To the right the view over Aylesbury Vale is spectacular; to the north can be seen the chateau-style Rothschild house which is now the Officers' Mess of RAF Halton, and immediately ahead the white buildings and chimneys of Stoke Mandeville Hospital. To the left the countryside drops away over the fields enclosing the small hamlets of Clanking and Smokey Row which nestle among them.

Carry on along the broad track through a small brake of woodland toward the Monument, crossing a deep sunken lane and through a gate on the other side. Now, at 827 ft, you have reached the highest point in the Chilterns, a blustery hilltop with the Monument standing majestically on its crown. It is worth having a look at this memorial to the local fallen in the Boer War. It was struck by lightning some 25 years ago and stone quarried in Cornwall was brought by ship from the tiny port of Newlyn to London and transported here for its repair. A more efficient conductor, it is hoped, will prevent this catastrophe from occuring again.

On a clear day the views from the hilltop are magnificent, looking right out over the Vale to the line of low hills encircling Aylesbury to

49

the north. To the left is the bold outline of Cymbeline's Mount with its isolated tree-clump on its bald crown and below it, sheltered amid a variety of colourful trees, is Chequers.

Walk past the Monument and, turning right, walk along the hill for 50 yards or so and then bear a little right on to a very narrow little path going downhill with Chequers ahead and Ellesborough Golf Course at the foot of the hill on the right. Walk above and parallel with the golf course. Follow the path as it turns right steeply downhill between trees to a track running along the valley at the bottom. Cross the track and go through the gate opposite and walk down the track ahead to a minor road. Turn right and cross the road; walk along the grass verge for 50 yards to take a marked footpath across a huge field. A first view of Ellesborough church, high on its man-made hillock, appears on the right over the trees. At the end of the path turn left onto a track and, after about 100 yards, turn right alongside a hedge just before a cottage on the left of the track - part of The Chequers estate. To the right, across another large field, Ellesborough church can now be clearly seen with a group of thatched cottages at its feet.

Where the path along the hedge joins the path across the field, turn left uphill to a stile and follow a small path, bearing slightly right, along the rounded lower slope of Cymbeline's Mount to Happy Valley, a beautiful dry valley full of trees of all shapes, colours and scents. Dry valleys often occur on the steep, chalky scarp slopes of the Chilterns and geologists believe that these were scoured through the chalk when the ice from the Ice Age thawed and torrents of water flooded down, some of it to form rivers like the Thames and other water to be absorbed so quickly by the chalk as to leave these deep, dry scores down the hills.

Follow the path down and up the hill through the head of the valley to emerge on to an open field where, on a clear day, the huge cooling towers of Didcot Power Station, some 20 miles away, may be seen a little to the left. Bear right at the far end of the field through a little brake of woodland and cross a metalled track (the tradesmen's entrance to Chequers) and take the stile opposite. Almost at once bear right down a small path through scrub and brambles to a stile, which cross and go uphill and then left along a path skirting the dry valley on the right. At its end climb the stile and turn right on to a track.

Follow the track as it bears left sharply uphill, then down and up across the dry moat of an Iron Age hill fort to the right. Stop here a moment to look back at the lovely valley and notice the variety and colour of the trees and shrubs tumbling down its side. Follow the path downhill past the hill fort to a stile in the trees and come down on to a track. Cross this, turning right and then, almost immediately, left at a Ridgeway sign to a stile, and cross into open countryside. Notice the deeply curving slope of the hill on the left as it meets the trees. This is Pulpit Hill and you will understand why when you see it!

Across this chalky downland follow the well-defined path and look out, in June particularly, for the many varieties of orchids to be found on the slope. The lovely little Chalk Blue butterfly is an inhabitant here, too. Ignore all side turnings and come down on to a deep track, which cross to follow the path straight ahead downhill, bearing left at the bottom on to a twisty little path which will bring you to a minor road. Turn left and cross the road to the lane leading to the *Plough* at Cadsden.

If you don't want to patronise the *Plough*, turn right on reaching the road and go on down it passing some pleasant houses on the right and Whiteleaf Golf Course on the left. At its junction with the A4010 at a roundabout, go straight across the roundabout with the *Black Horse* on the opposite corner and go on down the lane toward the hamlet of Askett. There are some pleasant thatched cottages on the left but the most memorable building is the tall, three-storied pub, the *Three Crowns*, which faces up the road. Just beside the *Three Crowns* turn right on to a footpath and go over a stile into a grass field. Follow the signposted footpath ahead over 2 stiles and across another field to yet another stile. Cross the field ahead to a stile in the righthand corner and another field to a stile to the left in the hedge. The kind landowners here have provided an excellent 'dog-exit' in the form of a woodblock slotted through three-sided brackets which can be lifted to allow the dog to scramble through and then dropped back into place through the brackets. The next stile, opposite, takes you on across a drive to another stile into a grass field and on to another stile. Here the yellow arrow signs of the North Bucks Way can be followed across fields and over stiles until some stabling on the left comes into view and there is an iron gate ahead. There is a stile alongside the gate! On the left is the delightful duck pond of Kimble Manor which lies a little uphill from the path on the right. Go past the Manor to a stile which comes down on to a minor road at Great Kimble. Turn right and walk up past the 'gentrified' old flint cottages typical of this area to the B4010.

Turn left at the road leaving St Nicholas' church on the righthand corner and walk along the footpath past the *Bernard Arms* toward Little Kimble. At the foot of the slope, cross the busy road to a lay-by. Walk along the lay-by pausing, perhaps, to study the little war memorial and then turn right into the B4010 signposted to Wendover, named Ellesborough Road. The 13th century All Saints church of Little Kimble lies on the right here. Walk up the road from the church until the footpath runs out opposite 'White Gates' and then cross to walk on the wide grass verge on the left. Cymbeline's Mount and the wooded slopes of Happy Valley can be seen away to the right.

At a sign indicating Ellesborough, take the marked footpath on the left over yet another stile and bear right to follow the path along the backs of gardens and across a large field, with Ellesborough church looming up on the right. Cross 3 bits of wooden fence on to a narrow metalled lane past 2 nice houses on the left. Cross the farm track at the end and follow the rough and overgrown path opposite over the fields to Butler's Cross. The Monument on top of Coombe Hill comes into view on the right. Having crossed 3 more stiles, the road through Butler's Cross is reached. Turn left and cross the road and, after 20 yards, take the marked footpath on the right and follow it ahead.

At a fence in what seems to be the middle of the path, take the path on the left and keep the fence on the right. Cross the next big field absolutely straight to a recently repaired stile in the hedge and cross the next field to a high stile into a grass field. Keep the hedge closely on the left and come down on to the drive of 16th century Wellwick House. Turn right on to the drive and, as you pass the house, pause to admire the splendid curlicues of the Tudor chimneys and the later, Jacobean, additions to the front elevation. Turn left to walk through the farmyard between old and new barns and, when the barns end, turn right along a path across a huge field. Cross a makeshift pretence of a stile in the lefthand corner at the start of a hedge into a grass field and, keeping the fence on the left, take the stile on the far side into another large field. Cross this diagonally on the usually well-defined path and then turn left at the field edge through the hedge to traverse the cricket field and over a railway footbridge back to the car.

Historical Notes

Cymbeline's Mount was the stronghold of the British King Cunobelin or Cymbeline from whom the villages of Great and Little Kimble derive their names. Relics found there indicate that this was the site of a Romano-British village and a Neolithic hill fort.

St Nicholas' church, Great Kimble is famous because it was into this church that John Hampden rode his horse to rouse the congregation into refusing to pay the Ship Tax in 1635. The 13th-14th century church is of flint and dressed stone and has a strikingly beautiful east window in gold and mauve made by Frankland Russell in 1844.

All Saints, Little Kimble is a small 13th century flint church set on a gentle slope just above the Lower Icknield Way (B4010). It houses the most impressive group of 14th century wall-paintings in the county. The paintings depict St Francis talking to the birds, St George and a Doom, St Katherine and St Bernard.

Chequers, the country home of successive Prime Ministers, was given for this purpose by its owner, Lord Lee of Fareham, in 1922. It lies in the parish of Ellesborough and successive Prime Ministers have attended divine service in the church of St Peter and St Paul there.

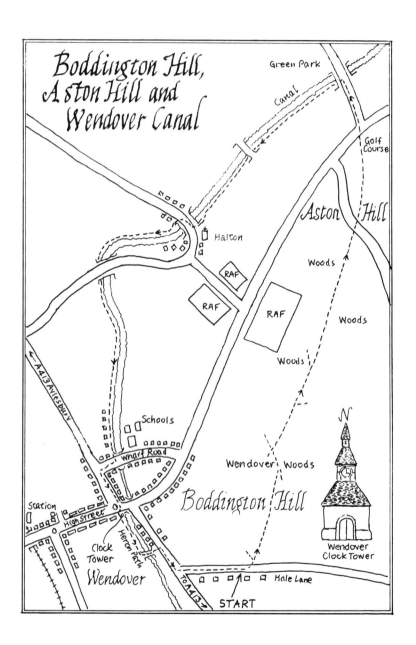

Boddington Hill,
Aston Hill and
Wendover Canal

Green Park

Canal

Golf Course

Aston Hill

Halton

Woods

RAF

RAF

RAF

Woods

Woods

Woods

A413 Aylesbury

Schools

Wharf Road

Wendover Woods

Station

Boddington Hill

High Street

Heron Path

Clock Tower

Wendover

N

Wendover Clock Tower

To A413

Hale Lane

START

Boddington Hill, Aston Hill and Wendover

Introduction: This is a walk with everything, from noble views, quiet, shady forest paths and wide spaces to a sight of kingfishers swooping along the canal and maybe a heron or two lurching awkwardly into the sky at the intrusion of humans on their territory. Much of it is through Forestry Commission land so the paths are well-defined and easy to follow, as is the towpath of the Wendover canal, the Wendover arm of the Grand Union, now a nature reserve which is managed by BBONT, the Berks, Bucks and Oxfordshire Naturalists' Trust. The walk ends with a stroll either through the charming little town of Wendover or along Heron Path, which leads from the town to the church and is now part of the Ridgeway. Iron Age forts can be seen along the route.

Distance: 9 miles - allow 3 to 4 hours for the walk; there is some quite steep climbing at first but the last few miles are on flat ground. OS Map Sheet 165 Aylesbury & Leighton Buzzard.

Refreshments: There are no pubs or restaurants on the walk but opposite the quaint Clock Tower in Wendover is a pleasant cafe where tea, coffee and snacks can be had all day. In Wendover High Street there are a number of pubs; the *Red Lion* on the left is 17th century and has an attractive arch through which visiting coaches entered the courtyard beyond. On the right are the *White Swan* and the *Two Brewers*. All these pubs serve both bar snacks and full meals. At the top of the High Street, where the A413 bears left for Amersham and London and the B4010 joins it at a roundabout, there are cafes on either side of the road. The Forestry Commission makes excellent provision for picnics en route with wooden benches and tables set out in open spaces. You are requested to take your litter home!

How to get there: From Amersham take the A413 for Aylesbury and about 10 miles from Amersham, just before Wendover, take a right fork signposted 'The Hale'. Go downhill past the *Wellhead Inn* and then uphill and, at the hill brow, take another right turn also signposted to The Hale. Go uphill on this for ½ mile and just after the brow of the hill park the car in a small, shady lay-by on the right opposite the wide wooden barrier of a Forestry Commission entrance. This parking place has been chosen deliberately to give the maximum of uphill walking at the start of the walk and the gentler walking at the end. It is possible to park the car in Wendover, at the railway station, or in the forest at the official car park but the walk is better routed if the Hale lay-by is used.

The Walk: Cross the road from the lay-by and take the marked footpath from the Forestry Commission entrance. After about 20 yards it is joined by another track coming in from the left but keep straight on up the hill, ignoring another track coming in from the left in about ¼ mile. On the right are badger tracks across the path coming between 2 large beech trees. The high bank on the left is bright with yellow wild potentilla in the spring and the purple-pink of rose-bay willow herb adorns it in the late summer. Sometimes the main track, which is a bridleway, becomes very muddy as it flattens out so a path has been made alongside it on the left, but do look out for hidden roots and stumps where the scrub has been cut away. At the top, after about ½ to ¾ mile of walking, the track ends in a gravelled T-junction. Turn left and, after 200 yards, turn right on to a vehicle track with wide grass verges which goes along the top of the forest. Below, on the left, lie the huge barrack blocks of RAF Halton and immediately ahead the village of Aston Clinton and the Wilstone Reservoir. To the right the hills arch round to Ivinghoe Beacon and Dunstable Downs. There are open spaces with picnic facilities along the track. To the left the wooded hills range on toward Princes Risborough.

Soon a new plantation appears on the left; it is mostly of conifers but wild cherry trees have been planted along its edge and their blossom is lovely to see in the spring. There are public tcilets on the left at the end of the track where it forms a junction with the main vehicle track through the forest. Here turn left and walk across the car park to bear right along the track past a 'No Entry' sign. After this sign the traffic is only one-way but keep a wary eye on the road as overhanging tree branches can obscure the view both of walkers and motorists. Use the grassy verge for preference.

After about ¾ mile cross a metalled road on the left going downhill and go straight on through another 'No Entry' sign. On the left in a little while evidence of the 1987 hurricane can be seen; shallow-rooted beeches fell in a sort of domino effect as the wind funnelled up the hill. Go round the gate into Halton Marches and, bearing slightly right at the white drive gate, go on to the road at Aston Hill. Here the view broadens out, rolling off downhill to the little town of Tring.

Cross the road and walk steeply downhill over grassland (marked 'Daniel's Trudge') and go down and up steps, all that remains of the moat of the Iron Age fort you have just walked across. Turn left at the top of the steps and take the wooded path ahead. Over the trees there is a splendid view of Tring Park, erstwhile home of Sir Frederick Rothschild, some of which now belongs to the Natural History Museum. The house itself is enclosed but the park is open to the public. Follow the path, ignoring side turnings, to the edge of the Chiltern Golf Course. Follow the path across the top of the course, past the clubhouse on the left and lovely rolling scenery on the right, to its far end, passing a metal drum-shaped structure and a shed to take the marked path between a hedge and a wire fence. Behind the hedge is a nature reserve called Ragpits where orchids can be found in June and primroses in the spring. The path drops downhill to a stile on to a quite busy road. Cross over and enter Stablebridge Road, going downhill to the canal bridge, so narrow that it is controlled by traffic lights. On the left side of the bridge descend to the towpath and turn left to walk along it. On the right is Green Park, once the home of Sir Anthony Rothschild but now a Recreational Training Centre run by the Bucks County Council. On the left is some rather scruffy woodland.

Under the next canal bridge Green Park is left behind and the scenery opens out to the wide expanses of the RAF playing fields on the left and a tiny airfield, used at one time for the training of aircraft engineers but now almost defunct except for light aircraft and glider use. Under another canal bridge the village of Halton comes into view and the towpath comes up to cross the road and descends to the right of the canal past a typical little canal-side cottage with a blue-painted fence. A few yards further on, sunk into the mud on the left bank of the canal, lies a fallen tree trunk which has the exact appearance of a basking crocodile. Here it is not unusual to see the pair of herons who inhabit this stretch of the canal; they sit like old grey gentlemen on the bankside or in the nearby field and flap clumsily away at the sight of people on the path. Ducks and moorhens bob in and out of the reeds bordering the water.

Soon, across the flat fields, the stubby tower of Weston Turville church can be seen rising above the trees on the right. Kingfishers ply this and the next bit of the canal. I have seen them more often on dull afternoons; I don't know if this means that they shun the sunshine for fishing or that their brilliant coloured plumage is easier to see when contrasted with a dull background. Go under a little iron bridge and, in the distance ahead, you will see the wooded hills you have just traversed. On the left is a large turning basin, now disused but once a busy mooring/turning space for the barges which brought London's sewage to manure the fields round

Wendover and, in the same barges, took back the grain grown in those same fields! Nowadays the turning basin is home to a pair of swans, some ducks and moorhens and an occasional gull. The water birds nest peacefully among the reeds on an island in the middle of the basin.

On down the towpath on the left are the playing fields of John Colet School and at the canal's edge is a newly constructed 'dipping' platform made by some stalwart parent volunteers so that the students could take water samples from the canal for analysis. There are two magnificent chestnut trees in the field on the right. Soon the path passes behind the gardens of one of Wendover's new housing estates and then, on the left bank, lies the old wharf. The water tumbles over a tiny fall from under the road beside the wharf. Notice, as you pass, the brave little campanula clinging for dear life to the brickwork and flowering madly throughout the summer.

Come up from the towpath on to the road and turn right here and walk straight down Wharf Road to its junction with the A413. Turn left at the bottom and cross Wharf Road into Aylesbury Road and walk along the path, shaded by lime trees on the right and passing, on either side of the road, pleasant examples of 17th, 18th and 19th century architecture. The grassy verge on this side of the road is called Manor Waste.

At the roundabout opposite the Clock Tower, a 19th century eccentricity, cross the Tring road with care and walk past the Clock Tower, which is now Wendover's Tourist Information Centre but opens only sporadically.

In front of you is Wendover High Street sloping gently uphill toward Coombe Hill, the highest point in the Chiltern range. If refreshment is required, this is just where to seek it, alcoholic or not!

If you are not minded to look for beer or tea, take the marked footpath ahead (Ridgeway) between metal bars and follow the Heron Path between the high wall of the old infant school and the backs of gardens, past a derelict Venture Scout Hut on the left and alongside a little stream. On the right is a cricket field known as The Witchell. Legend has it that this was to have been the site of the 13th century church of St Mary the Virgin but, as fast as the foundations were laid, so the fairies came and removed them to a place some ¼ mile further along the path. The builders finally gave in, the fairies won and St Mary's is still about a mile from the town's centre. Walk past an elegant white house called Bucksbridge House and cross the small road on to the ropewalk with Heron Path House on the left and part of Hampden Meadow on the right. It was along this part of Heron Path that ropes, locally made, were stretched and plaited.

Facing the path is a small house called Sluice Cottage and beside it, to the left, is a narrow bridge over the stream by a tiny weir. Cross the bridge and take the footpath winding uphill through the scrub and past some lovely gardens to the road, Hale Road. Here turn right and walk along the path for about 50 yards, then cross the road with care on the hillbrow to take the lane up to The Hale on the left and walk the ½ mile back up the hill to the parked car.

Historical Notes

Boddington Hill and Aston Hill both have Iron Age forts on top of them, the one in the forest to the left of the main path and the other on the green top of Aston Hill. It would be easy not to notice either! Coming nearer the present day, a motor car manufacturer called Martin used Aston Hill for racing and testing his cars - hence the Aston Martin.

Halton House: Described by Eustace Balfour as a combination of French chateau and gambling house, with its extensive grounds along the lower wooded slopes of the Chilterns here, the house was built for Baron Alfred de Rothschild in 1884 by W.R. Rogers and has a splendidly ornate interior including a gigantic crystal chandelier in its entrance hall. The property was acquired by the Crown on the death of Baron Alfred in 1918 and is now the Officers' Mess of RAF Halton. The barracks, workshops and hospital straggle through the woodland from Halton to Wendover. The little church of St Michael is not much older than the house for it was rebuilt by Henry Rhodes in 1813. There is one medieval relic, a brass with kneeling figures of Henry Bradschaw, Chief Baron of the Exchequer until his death in 1553, with his wife and children.

Wendover is a pretty little town whose centre still preserves much of the charming 17th and 18th century buildings of which it is justifiably proud despite a great deal of new building on its outskirts dribbling off toward Aylesbury. The quaint Clock Tower is a 19th century folly while on the left side of the Tring road lies a row of thatched cottages which were part of Henry VIII's marriage settlement with Anne Boleyn and these are, naturally, named Boleyn Cottages.

Famous names associated with Wendover are John Hampden and Edmund Burke who were Wendover's Parliamentary representatives in 1623 and 1796 respectively. The ill-famed 'Hanging' Judge Jeffreys stayed at Wellwick House on his way to Assizes at Aylesbury.

The 17th century *Red Lion* in the High Street has hosted such famous men as Oliver Cromwell, Robert Louis Stevenson and the poet, Rupert Brooke.

Wendover has 2 mills, both now converted to housing. The tower mill, on the Aylesbury road, is the home of a music publisher who can sometimes be seen, and heard, practising the ancient Scottish mouth music from the ledge of the now sail-less mill.

Wendover, The Lee and Swanbottom

Introduction: This very pretty and scenic walk can easily be joined on to the Chartridge one (Walk 13) and offers then a good day's walking of around 20 miles, through beautiful farmland and woodland scenery and some attractive villages. As a pleasant, not too demanding, walk it can well stand on its own. Parts of the Ridgeway are traversed and the villages of The Lee and Swanbottom are picturesque and colourful.

Distance: 7 or 9 miles. There is both a short and a longer route through Wendover Forest on offer - allow about 3 hours for the shorter walk. OS Map Sheet 165 Aylesbury & Leighton Buzzard.

Refreshments: The *Cock and Rabbit* at The Lee has an excellent reputation for good food; it has a restaurant as well as bar meals. The *Well Head*, at the start of the walk, also serves good bar food. The *Gate* at Swanbottom has a pleasant open garden equipped with tables and benches and serves good, plentiful food and traditional ales.

How to get there: Leave Amersham by the A413 towards Aylesbury and in 9 miles look out for a right fork signposted 'The Hale'. Take this fork and drive down the lane for ¼ mile passing the *Well Head* inn on the right. Just past the pub and a cream-painted, gabled cottage is a track on the right. Turn up the track (Ridgeway) and park the car on the grass verge on the left after 50 yards, almost opposite the farm buildings on the right.

It is quite simple to take this walk from a train journey to Wendover. Walk up Station Approach and turn left at the top into Pound Street. At the roundabout turn right into South Street and, just past a large garage on the left, take the field path on the left diagonally across the field to a gate and then across a road and into another field, Hampden Meadow, and go over it. Go on to the path to pass the pond at the end of the meadow and on to Church Lane which curves right round the church. Follow this to its T-junction and cross with care onto the Ridgeway beside the gabled cottage opposite. Trains run every hour from Marylebone and the journey takes 50 minutes.

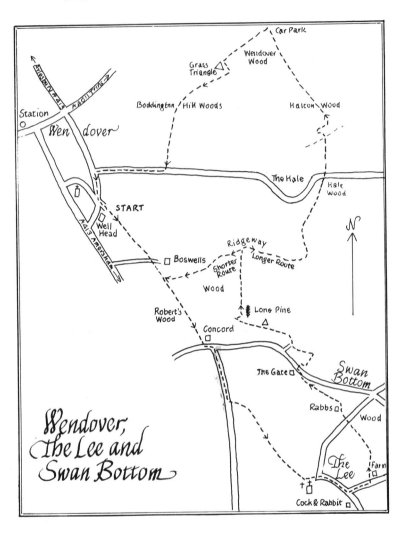

The Walk: Follow the Ridgeway path straight ahead for ¾ mile, past farm buildings and cottages on the left and, in a small enclosure on the right, 6 very handsome geese who stand to attention to glower at the passerby. Soon, on the left, is the entrance to Boswells and on the right the splendid avenue of trees forming its driveway. Go on past the house to a point where the path divides and here take the extreme righthand path. After 20 yards or so climb the bank on the right by a narrow path and turn left to walk parallel with and above the sunken lane, Hogtrough.

To the right is a sloping field which soon gives way to woodland. This is Robert's Wood and is a nature reserve dedicated to Sir Robert Barlow who owned the land. Watch out for narrow badger tracks leaving and entering the wood. Badgers always use the same route when they forage at night and their tracks become well worn. Often deer can be seen here. The reserve is now managed by the Bucks County Naturalists Trust. The high path is usually cleaner than the sunken lane as it is not supposed to be used by horse riders but, sadly, some equestrians seem to have little thought for their fellow country-lovers and it is often very churned up and muddy at its far end.

At the second wooden barrier bear left on to the, more or less, metalled lane opposite a farm entrance and follow the lane past a white cottage on to the road. Turn left on to the road and then almost immediately right into another narrow lane alongside a white house on the right. In the autumn, scarlet trusses of viburnum berries make a brilliant splash of colour in the hedge. On the right is a wide view of the whole valley to the hills on the other side, the only eyesore being the hideous pylons which stride across the valley bottom. Peaceful cattle graze on the left behind a tall hedge of hazel, thorn and oak.

After ½ mile, at a pleasant cottage painted blue and white, cross the stile in the hedge on the left and cross the field diagonally to a stile in the far right corner. Go over the stile and turn left along a path and, at the wood edge, turn right to follow the path over the fields alongside the wood, between fields and then more woods and more fields for ½ to ¾ mile to an open area with a farm track running across it. Cross the track to the stile opposite and walk across the field toward the farm buildings to the right. There is a very old, beautiful barn among them.

Go over the stile in the corner by the farmhouse and across the drive to another stile. Over this stile walk the 10 yards or so across the top of the field to a stile into the churchyard, where there are 2 churches. One is very old and the other, a Victorian building, was erected by the Liberty family of The Lee. Turn right out of the churchyard on to a lane and then left alongside the village green, past a row of charming cottages, much 'done up' in recent years. Notice the cairn of pudding stones on the green. This is a mixture of very hard stones, annealed at the thawing of the Ice Age and bundled together in the resultant torrents of water to give an appearance exactly of a plum-pudding. On the right of the green is the *Cock and Rabbit*.

If the walk is to continue to Chartridge, cross the green at The Lee to the *Cock and Rabbit* and the road running alongside it. Cross the road ahead onto a gravelled track opposite and follow this as for the Chartridge walk.

For the present walk bear left at the end of the green and, after ¼ mile, take a not very obvious signposted footpath through a tangly thicket on the left which goes between the farmhouse and the farmyard to a fence. Go over the fence and follow the path downhill to a stile into a field. Keeping the fence/hedge on the left, follow the path across the field to the wood edge. Go over the stile and follow the path through the wood, to 'Rabb's'. Turn right after passing a cottage and its garden and follow the path along the side of the field keeping the hedge on the right. Keep to the right at the fork in the path on entering the wood ahead. Go over the stile at the end of the wood and cross the field in front, over another stile and then down the track ahead to the *Gate* public house.

Cross the lane at the *Gate*, turn right and then almost at once turn left on to a track passing a group of cottages on the left. Soon the path makes a sharp bend to the right; here turn left on to a small path into the wood and then left again onto a more obvious path. Keep on this path along the wood edge to a T-junction where another, broader track joins. Here turn right and, after 50 yards, turn left again. Ignore the track on the right and keep ahead for ¼ mile (Bench Mark on right), emerging from the wood into a new plantation with crossing tracks. Turn right and walk alongside the plantation for 30 yards to a pine tree standing high and on its own. Go left beside it at the Y-junction. There is a good mix of young trees, beech, oak and conifer, on each side of the track which goes to the conifer wood ahead and downhill to meet the old Ridgeway at a T-junction.

(For a SHORT CUT, turn left at this T-junction and walk downhill on the Ridgeway, ignoring a track coming in on the left. There are tantalising glimpses of the rolling countryside through the trees on the right as the hillside drops sharply away. Bear left with the path at the bottom of the hill and turn right onto the track in 50 yards and you are back on the track from which you started, ¾ mile from the car.)

Turn right and follow the well-trodden track along the contour of the hill, ignoring all side turnings for about 1 mile. Be warned, parts of this bit of the Ridgeway are nearly always muddy because small springs emerge along the hillside from the chalky subsoil. Go round the deep pudding basin formed by the hills, in the centre of which lies Wendover. You may very well come upon tiny muntjac deer up here and may well hear, or even see, the peacocks which inhabit nearby Uplands Farm.

Carry on along the route till a small, deeply sunken lane is reached and cross it to follow the Ridgeway on the other side (right then left).

The path is marked with an arrow and a yellow acorn and the entrance to Uphill Farm is opposite.

Follow the path along the edge of the ancient beechwood with glimpses of farm buildings on the right and, deep in the hollow on the left, is Hale Farm. There are magnificent views over the patchwork of fields, broken by clumps of trees and hedges, to the tree-clad hills in the distance. The landscape falls sharply away at your feet to the left to grassy fields below. Keep up to the right following the wood edge and then follow the path as it bears left alongside a field with a hedge on the right. There are 2 deep old chalk-pits on the left. The path ends at a T-junction with another sunken lane. Cross this - down and up the other side - and then turn right onto an obvious path and through a barred gateway. Follow this path until it emerges onto the gravelled road through the forest.

Here walk straight ahead along the grass verge of the road for ¾ mile, ignoring all side turnings. Comfortable farmland stretches away to the left while dense forest hides the view on the right. After ¾ mile the main forest car park is reached and here, just before the car park, turn left where there is a stone plaque commemorating the 1970 Countryside Award won for the good management of the forest. There are toilets on the right among the trees. Carry on down this road for another ½ mile, walking on the wide grass verge as cars travel both ways here. There is a pleasant plantation of young trees on the left which has been interspersed with flowering cherry and looks lovely in the spring. On the left are long views of the wooded hills on the other side of the bowl where you have just been walking. On the right is a viewpoint right out over the Vale of Aylesbury to the shallow hills in the north. Directly below is the little reservoir at Weston Turville with the white buildings of Stoke Mandeville Hospital behind it and, over on the right, the hideous tower of Bucks County Council offices, known locally as HMS Aylesbury.

At a humpy triangle of grass turn left and follow a path slightly downhill for 200 yards. Turn right onto a broad, and sometimes muddy, bridleway and keep on this, steadily downhill, past the back of a large house and ignoring all side turnings, to emerge onto a minor road where turn right. Follow the road to a T-junction and turn left (there is a footpath on the other side of the road) and then after about ¼ mile left again into the track by a pillar box and the gabled cottage to find the car.

Historical Notes

The Lee: There are 2 churches in 1 churchyard at The Lee. The older of the 2, a simple rectangle of stone with a huge porch, is of 12th century origin while the newer, red brick church of St John the Baptist, was built by Augustus Frere in 1867 and later embellished in Edwardian style by S.F. Prynne in 1911. On a bend in the road toward Great Missenden is a goggle-eyed figurehead standing in the front garden of 'Pipers', the home of the Stewart-Liberty family. It is of Admiral Howe and was bought by the family from the ship of that name when the ship was broken up.

The Ridgeway path in the Chilterns is, strictly speaking, the immeasurably older track, the Icknield Way, a prehistoric chalk route which ran on over Dunstable Downs to Cambridgeshire and East Anglia. The Countryside Commission has marked a continuous track of some 80 miles from Overton in Wiltshire to Ivinghoe Beacon in Buckinghamshire and called it The Ridgeway Path. Parts of this ancient track are walked here. The Upper Icknield Way was the winter route when flooded valleys made the lower route, the Lower Icknield Way, impassable. No one knows from whence comes the name Icknield; it is so old it has no known lingual root and must derive from the forgotten language of our unknown ancestors.

Cobbler's Hill
and Great Hampden

Introduction: This lovely part of the Chilterns could be termed a walker's paradise; numerous paths and lanes run down the hillsides to the fertile valleys with their small 'spring-line' villages and wind up from the valleys to the hilltop 'forts' on either side. The views of gentle, peaceful farmland backed by the dark shades of woodlands, mostly beech, the fields frilled against the trees, with a white outline of the chalky outcrop, cannot fail to appeal to the eye. Closer inspection reveals the presence of a variety of wild and semi-wild life. Pheasants, rabbits and deer can often be seen. Tall hedges of elder, dog-rose and thorn are bordered in summer by a profusion of heavily-scented cow parsley. In spring, primroses and dog violets clamber about the banks and bluebells fill the woods with a veritable cloud of blue. Small farmhouses and cottages nestle in the folds of the hills.

The walk starts at Cobbler's Hill, high above Cockshoots Wood and winds down a lane to King's Beech, oddly named because it is, in fact, 2 oak trees set on a triangle of grass! The walk then climbs up to the edge of Prestwood and across the fields and lanes to Great Hampden, down and up to the hamlet of Little Hampden and from there through quite spectacular landscape down and up again through the beechwoods back to Cobbler's Hill.

Distance: 7 or 5 miles - please don't rush through this beautiful walk; allow time to pause and look back at the views. The short walk will need 2 hours or so, the longer up to 3 hours. There is some quite steep uphill work to do. OS Map Sheet 165 Aylesbury & Leighton Buzzard.

Refreshments: There are 2 pubs en route; the *Hampden Arms* at Hampden Row and the *Rising Sun* at Little Hampden. Both open their doors at 12 noon and 7pm and neither landlord is enamoured of muddy boots on the premises so these should be removed before entering. Both have pleasant gardens in which to sit on a sunny day and both provide excellent bar meals and snacks.

How to get there: From the A413 Amersham to Aylesbury road, almost equidistant between Wendover and Great Missenden, take an unclassified

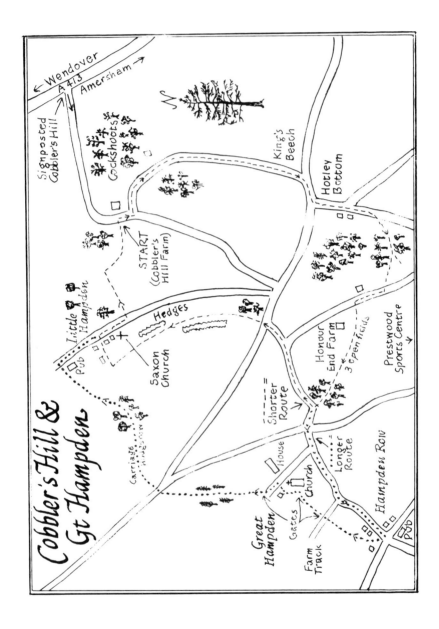

lane clearly signposted Cobbler's Hill. It is on the right coming from Wendover and on the left from Great Missenden. Drive uphill carefully on the winding single-track lane to Cobbler's Hill Farm at the top and park on the left of the lane opposite the wide farm entrance.

The Walk: Turn left and go on down the lane past the farm buildings. Take the left fork at the division, bearing left and then right to follow the lane downhill, passing a pleasant house set back on the left and sweeping views of ploughland and beechwoods all around. In September and October this is real pheasant country and dozens of them will hurry across the lane or rise, screeching and flapping, from the hedge bottoms.

At the far end of the lane is a T-junction at King's Beech with an unclassified but quite busy little road. Turn right and cross the road, and after 100 yards, turn left into Hotley Bottom Lane and, after another 200 yards, take the right fork into Greenlands Lane by some typical flint cottages and a farmhouse.

Follow the lane steeply uphill with woodland on the left and passing a nice house and garden on the right. Take the next, marked, footpath on the right, through a gate, across a field, through another gate and over a stile into a wood. In the spring look out for the magnificent wisteria clambering over the pretty house on the right as you cross the field.

Follow the path into the wood, bearing left at the fork and go over a stile at the wood's edge on to another unclassified lane, turning right to walk down it. Prestwood Sports Centre lies back on the left and there is a pretty thatched cottage on the right. After about ⅓ mile, just after the 'Road Narrows' sign on the road on the left, take the marked footpath on the left and follow it straight ahead over 3 open fields with Honour End Farm lying on the right and marvellous views toward the wooded hills all around. At the end of the third field cross a stile into a narrow path with mixed woods on the right and open fields to the left and follow this till it emerges, over a stile, on to a lane.

If you are following the MAIN WALK, turn left and follow the road across the crossroads. Bear sharply left then right as it makes its way to Hampden Row - a group of cottages, a cricket field and a pub - *The Hampden Arms* - on the left. If you are taking the SHORT CUT, continue at * below.

At the *Hampden Arms*, cross the road and take the track opposite between the colourful gardens of the cottages and on to an open field. Cross this field straight ahead and go across a metalled farm track to a gate on the far side. Go through the gate and follow the well-defined path across the fields, keeping the fence on the left and making for Great Hampden church. Go through a little gate to get into the churchyard and follow the path to the left, leaving the church on the right, and turn left on to the drive of Hampden House. On the left is the splendidly tall Tudor stable block and, on the right, the house itself more or less hidden from view by trees. Just past the house go through the white gate ahead onto a grass track and immediately over a stile on the right into a grass field. Here there is an excellent view of the long south front of the 15th century battlemented house. It has recently been extensively restored, stucco removed and the old warm red brick revealed.

Follow the field path across the front of the house through a plantation of conifers on the left and mixed woodland on the right. The path descends gently to 2 stiles which are crossed to enter a cultivated field. Cross this field diagonally; the path is always clearly reinstated by the farmer after ploughing so it is well-defined but can be muddy. Across the valley to the right can be seen the warm red brick of the timber-framed farmhouse. The path emerges onto the road over a stile.

Cross the road to the gate opposite with a Public Footpath sign against it and go onto the track, Carriage Hedgerow, leading up through the beechwoods, decked with bluebells in the spring. After about ⅓ mile take a small path to the right (watch out for the white arrow footpath signs to indicate this, painted on a tree) and go through the wood edge to another stile and a well-defined path across a cultivated field. Pause here to look back over the valley at the wonderful patchwork of fields, plantations and mixed woodland on the far side. At the top of the field the path creeps through the hedge to a stile. Over the stile there is a small area of conifers and scrub and the path leads to another stile. Go over the stile and follow the path diagonally across a cultivated field, which is littered with large, clumsily-shaped flints. Cross the track at the top of the field and follow a signposted grass path opposite between an orchard on the left and a cottage and garden on the right. The path emerges on the lane above the *Rising Sun*. Turn right down the lane to Manor Farm on the left and carry on with the walk as described at ** below.

*If the thought of a pub lunch at the *Hampden Arms* doesn't appeal to you, turn right instead of left at this point and follow the lane steeply downhill between woods of beech, rowan and Spanish chestnut. Walk with care as motorists use the winding lane. Shortly there is a lane coming in on the right which ignore but, having crossed it, pause to look to right and left at the splendid avenue, mostly of lime trees, which is reputed to have been planted in honour of a visit to Hampden House by Queen Elizabeth I. The house can be seen at the top of the avenue to the left. The avenue leads downhill on the right to the road running through the valley bottom and, at the entrance, are 2 unusually shaped lodges known as the Pepper Boxes. Go on down the original lane to the road at the bottom of the hill and cross it with care. Take the marked path opposite to the right of a small brake of conifers. The path rises quite steeply uphill and, in summer, the hedges are a riot of colour with dog roses, scabious, cow parsley and willowherb blooming abundantly. Keep the hedge on the left and walk up alongside an open field which, in autumn, clatters with the rise of the many pheasants departing at the appearance of humans and, in winter, provides a sports ground for hares.

After about ⅓ mile the path suddenly sneaks through a gap in the hedge; watch out for this as it is easy to miss but there is an arrow indicating the direction on a telegraph pole on the far side of the hedge. Now go on uphill with the hedge on the right following the contour of the field. Across the field on the right is the tiny 15th century church at Little Hampden with 3 tall larches beside it. New cherry trees have been planted along the edge of the path and their blossom is a delight in the spring.

Where a track crosses the path turn right and walk past the picturesque old farmhouse to the road. Here turn left if you wish for refreshments at the *Rising Sun*, which is about ¼ mile away on the left. Otherwise turn right on to the road, and rejoin the main walk.

**Turn left off the road on to a footpath alongside Manor Farm leaving the hotch-potch of farm buildings, old and new, on the left.

Follow the path down and up hill across the fields to the wood edge where you can turn round for a splendid view of the rolling countryside, circling the valley you have just crossed.

Carry on through the wood along the uphill path as it bears left and then right, climbing more and more steeply alongside a new plantation of beech and conifer on the left and on through the wood to open fields between wire fences. Go through a metal gate at the end of the path and walk along the side of Cobbler's Hill Farm to the lane and the car parked opposite.

Historical Notes

The Church of St Mary Magdalen, Great Hampden is of flint with some stone facing and has a clerestoried 13th century nave. Unfortunately the church is kept locked as a precaution against vandalism as it houses an intriguing monument to John Hampden, who died in 1643 after wounds sustained at Chalgrove Field during the Civil War. The monument, designed for his grandson by Henry Cheere in 1743, is of 2 cherubs, one of whom appears to be waving a funny hat, seated on a sarcophagus surmounted by a large oval medallion depicting the Battle of Chalgrove Field.

71

Great Hampden House, as it stands today, is a heavily Gothicised 18th century house but it has been the site of the manor house since the 11th century and the home of successive Hampdens, Earls of Buckingham. Set in a high downland park, surrounded by beechwoods and arable fields, the house commands a majestic view of the valley which divides the 2 Hampdens. It was at one time the home of John Hampden, cousin of Oliver Cromwell. He is famous for his refusal to pay the notorious Ship Tax imposed by Charles I. It is said that he rode his horse one Sunday morning down through Carriage Hedgerow and up the hill to Kimble church, where he rode into the church during Morning Prayer and disrupted the service to rally his tenants to follow his example. The last Earl of Buckingham to live in the house was a much-loved and respected 'Squire' known to all the villagers and who knew them by name also. A great cricket enthusiast, in 1950 he organised the laying of a cricket pitch beyond the *Hampden Arms*, which is kept immaculately.

The Lee, Chesham
and Chartridge

Introduction: From the old market town of Chesham, the Chiltern ridges strike uphill like the outstretched fingers on an open hand; Chartridge, Hawridge, Ashridge, Pednor, Hundridge. Between the ridges deep dry valleys are scoured down the landscape and this walk takes in some ridges and some valleys, but there is only very little steep climbing since the walk, starting off at The Lee, sets off on high ground. It is quite simple to walk on the extra mile or so into Chesham, the path leading on through pleasant parkland to descend into the town close to St Mary's church.

Distance: 10 or 12 miles; a pleasant day's walking. OS Map Sheet 165 Aylesbury & Leighton Buzzard.

Refreshments: The *Cock and Rabbit* at The Lee and the *Bell* at Chartridge both offer bar meals, and the former has a restaurant with a justifiably good reputation locally.

How to get there: From the A413, about 2 miles north-west of Great Missenden, take an unclassified single track road called Leather Lane. There are indications of a right turn on the A413 coming from Amersham via the Great Missenden bypass. At the top of Leather Lane turn left and bear right where another lane enters. Soon you will notice a magnificent figurehead glowering at you over the hedge on the right. Turn left alongside the *Cock and Rabbit* and park the car opposite the green beyond the pub.

The Walk: Retrace the route past the *Cock and Rabbit* and cross the road to a track opposite. Walk down this for ¼ mile past some excellent barn restorations on the left. At the end of the hedge, 200 yards past the wall on the left, take a path on the left over a stile into mixed woodland, bearing right. Follow this track through the wood, out into open country at the foot of Lee Common and back into woods to emerge, after about 1 mile, over a stile on to the road at Ballinger Bottom. Cross

73

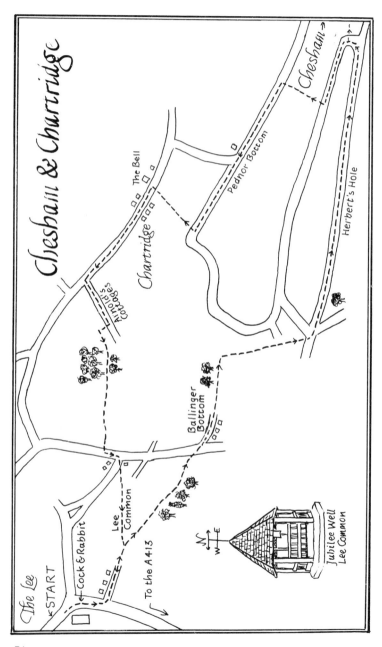

Chesham & Charridge

Chesham →

Chesham →

Pednor Bottom

The Bell

Herbert's Hole

Charridge

Arnold's Cottages

Ballinger Bottom

Lee Common

Jubilee Well
Lee Common

Cock & Rabbit

The Lee
←START

To the A413

the road and bear right up the marked track and, where it divides after some 50 yards, take the extreme right fork into the woods with the back gardens of some houses on the right. This is marked as a footpath but riders do use it so it can be muddy in wet weather. Unusually, among the predominant beeches, there are many oaks and holly bushes here. Notice the funny little red Wendy house on stilts at the end of one of the gardens and the lovely glow of light through the tall, straight beech trunks on the left.

Keep on this track to a stile into a field. Cross the stile and, keeping close to the hedge on the right, walk across the top of the field to the stile in the hedge in the far right corner - designed, one might think, to put one off as it is invaded by prickly holly bushes on both sides. Cross the stile and proceed down the field ahead, keeping the hedge now on the left. At the end of the field cross another stile and turn left. Go through a gate and immediately right into a lane.

Where the lane makes a sharp right bend, keep straight on over a stile onto a marked footpath with a tall hedge on the right and a field on the left. Go over stiles and down a field on to another lane. Here turn left and take the right fork on to a broad track along the foot of the valley, Herbert's Hole.

Walk here through mixed woodland on the right and open country on the left. Soon, through a gate, the wood is left behind and there is open, undulating countryside all around, the skyline broken from time to time by tall hedges and small brakes of trees. Follow this well-used track for about 1½ miles. In summer it is bordered by a variety of wild flowers; the pungently heavy scent of cow-parsley predominates. In the autumn there is a particularly attractive dark blue vetch which grows in clumps about halfway along. It is worth having a look at the old wooden barn on the left to notice the beautiful structure of the old beams, though it now has a rather derelict air and a corrugated iron roof! A large notice proclaims that model aircraft are flown from here and warns the pedestrian to beware.

At a gate at the end of the track turn left on to a small lane and soon, on the right, is the marked footpath up steps through the hedge, to Chesham through Lowdnes Park. If you don't want to visit Chesham go on up the lane, bearing left and uphill and, after about ½ mile, take an unmarked track alongside a hedge to Pednor Bottom. A rusty, lopsided corrugated iron shed will identify this rather obscure path. The outskirts of Chesham can be seen on the hill and in the valley to the right.

At the lane at Pednor Bottom turn left and walk along the lane for about 1½ miles, ignoring the lane coming in from the right. The footpath is about ¾ mile further on past this lane just before it makes a sharp left hand bend. It is unmarked but there is a Public Footpath sign on the left side of the lane opposite it and it is found on the right side of a formidably wired metal gate. It is narrow, steep and overgrown but doesn't last long. At the top of the untidy path is a stile into a field. Cross this and, keeping the hedge on the left, go across the field to a stile in the left hand corner. Cross the stile and take the track ahead. After 20 yards, just before a farmhouse, turn right and go over a stile to follow the marked path across a field, bearing slightly right and emerge, over a stile, on to the Chartridge road opposite *The Bell*.

Turn left and follow this quite busy little road for a short ¼ mile and then turn left again into Cogdells Lane. After 100 yards take a marked path on the right over the playing fields opposite Arnolds Cottages. Go straight ahead along a well-trodden path over cultivated fields and into a grass field, keeping close to the hedge on the right when it is reached. There are fine views over Pednor Bottom to Great Hundridge Manor on the ridge on the left and some pleasant houses across the fields on the right. Go over a makeshift stile and across the next field to a stile opposite. Here cross a track and go over a rickety stile to take the path opposite. Go across the field to a stile in the hedge on the right.

Over this stile, turn left toward a wood with the hedge now on the left. Go into the wood over a stile and follow the narrow little path against the wire fence on the left downhill along the wood edge. Cross the track at the bottom and follow a marked path, more or less straight ahead, through the wood and uphill, following arrows round an old chalk pit. At the wood edge cross a track and a stile into a field. Here there are marvellous open views to the left, especially in the autumn, when the colours of the trees form a spectacular backdrop to the rolling fields.

Keeping the hedge on the right, go across the field to a grassy track between hedges. There are 6 more stiles to climb over in the next ¼ mile on to a lane. Turn left at the lane and walk along for about 50 yards and turn right into the lane signposted to Lee Common. There is an off-licence and a shop on the left and, on the right, a rather superior roofed well set up by the residents of Lee Common to mark Queen Victoria's Jubilee in 1897.

Follow the lane round a sharp right bend just after the well and some pretty whitewashed cottages and take the marked path on the left over the allotments opposite St Mary's Close. Go through the gate on the far side and cross a lane to a stile and down a small field to another stile. On the far side of this stile cross Lee Common to another one diagonally opposite at the foot of the hill. Turn right and follow the original path back through the wood, left and then right, to the track to The Lee.

Historical Notes

The Lee is a small hamlet surrounding a triangular village green on which a 'cairn' of pudding-stone rests. These stones, like Sarsen stones, erupted from the earth's crust at the end of the Ice Age and are composed of an amalgam of resistant types of stone of various shapes and colours, giving them very much the appearance of a plum pudding. There are other stones of this type in Wendover and Chesham.

There are 2 churches in 1 churchyard here. The old, 12th century, church is a simple rectangle with a tiled roof and a large porch while the new church of St John the Baptist was built beside it in 1867. The chancel, with oak linenfold panelling, was added in 1911 by S.F. Pryne at the behest of the Liberty family who lived in the manor and, as the name implies, are the owners of Liberty's stores in Regent Street.

The ship's figurehead in the grounds of Piper's is that of Admiral Howe and graced the ship of that name until 1860 when the ship was broken up. The Liberty family bought it and the timber from the ship was used in the rebuilding of the store in the 1920s.

Chesham: The little town is sited in a sheltered valley at the source of the river Chess, which divides here into separate channels and must have been the reason for settlements in Roman and, indeed, Saxon times. Around the Norman church of St Mary are some charming 17th and 18th century houses, particularly that built for William Lowdnes in 1712, the Bury, a tall brick house with quoins and a parapet.

77

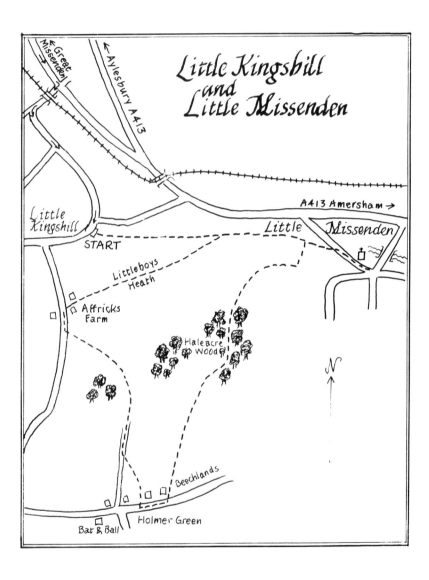

WALK FOURTEEN

Little Kingshill
and Little Missenden

Introduction: This short walk starts from Little Kingshill, traversing a spine of the hills with splendid open views on each side and enters the delightful tiny village of Little Missenden, which seems to have been bypassed by time. The return route is through Haleacre Wood and across Little Boys Heath.

Distance: 4 miles - a pleasant afternoon walk.

If you want to leave the car behind and take the train to Great Missenden, this is simply done. The station lies a few yards uphill, almost opposite the road from the roundabout to which you would have driven in the car. Walk down the station approach, turn right into the High Street and follow the directions as given. This will add another 5 miles to the walk but may well also add to your enjoyment of it! OS Map Sheet 165 Aylesbury & Leighton Buzzard.

Refreshments: There are 2 pubs in Little Missenden village, both of which serve bar snacks. They are the *Crown*, near the manor house and the *Red Lion* at the far end of the village. The *Bat and Ball* at Holmer Green is halfway round the walk.

How to get there: From the A413 Amersham to Aylesbury road (7 miles from Amersham and 10 from Aylesbury) take the turning for Great Missenden at a roundabout and follow the road for ¼ mile to a T-junction with the High Street. Turn left down this narrow busy street and out at the far end. Follow the same road for approximately 1 mile and turn right alongside the *Nag's Head* public house, signposted to Little and Great Kingshill. Follow the lane, Nag's Head Lane, as it curves sharply left uphill under a railway bridge. At the top of the hill the lane takes a sharp right turn and, just past this turn beyond a bus stop on the left, is a large lay-by where you can park the car.

The Walk: Turn left and follow the marked path through trees and out, over a stile, into open fields where the clearly defined path strides ahead along the ridge, with beautiful countryside falling and rising again on either side. The call of larks is predominant up here in the fields and greenfinches nest in the thick hedge ahead.

Go through the hedge and over a stile into the next field and follow the path, bordered in summer by the rich blue flowers of chicory, to a pair of stiles on either side of a steeply sunken lane. Cross both stiles into a big paddock and walk toward the buildings in the right hand corner, where there is a stile on to the road into the village of Little Missenden.

On the left is the tiny river Misbourne which is, more often than not, dried up but, in the spring, the grassy verge of the field is a carpet of palest white snowdrops. The church lies a little back from the road on the left and, if you are fortunate enough to encounter a flower-arranger or a 'Holy Duster' inside, the church is well worth a look round.

Follow the village road past the church to find the beautiful Jacobean manor house on the left, seen through high wrought-iron gates. Keep on down the road, ignoring turnings to right and left if you wish for refreshment at one of the pubs. If not, retrace your steps through the village to the stile into the paddock, now on the left just past the houses. Recross the paddock to the sunken track and turn left over the stile on to it.

This very ancient track meanders uphill between high hedges of hazel and thorn into Haleacre Wood, a large area of mixed woodland across the hillside. The path emerges from the wood out into open country again, between hedges with wide grass fields on both sides. Follow the path to farm buildings on the right and on to a lane where you turn right at the edge of Holmer Green village. The *Bat and Ball* lies about 400 yards ahead on the left.

Just after the farmhouse and a flint and brick house called 'Beechlands', turn right on to a waymarked footpath, go over a stile and across a large field, bearing slightly left to a stile in the far left hand corner. Go over the stile and, keeping the hedge on the left, walk down the field to another stile. Go over this stile and turn right to take the flinty track downhill between a hedge on the left and the other side of Haleacre Wood on the right, ignoring all side turnings. The path climbs the last bit uphill to Affrick's Farm.

Turn right, almost doubling back on your tracks, on to the farm road. Walk through between the farm buildings and on, past the end of the metalled track, to a grassy path ahead. Go through 2 gates to a stile in the hedge. Over the stile turn left and, keeping the hedge always on the left, walk down and then uphill over Little Boys Heath to the original path along the ridge. Turn left and follow the path back through the trees to the lay-by and the car.

Historical Notes

Little Missenden: The church of St John the Baptist is of 12th and 13th century origin but in the 14th century the north chapel was added and the timbered porch in the 15th century, so it is a hotch-potch of periods. There are some interesting wall paintings of the 13th century, in particular one of St Christopher with the Child Jesus and fish around his feet, and one of St Katherine.

In October each year the village holds a Festival of Arts and the works of such contemporary composers as Michael Tippett and Edmund Rubbra are performed. Both these composers had close connections with Little Missenden Abbey which, before the Second World War, was a school for 'difficult' children. The school was run by Mrs Lister-Kaye, a child psychologist, on the lines of A.S. Neill's school in Sussex. Michael Tippett taught at the school for a short time and Edmund Rubbra, whose piano was housed in the school hall, was a frequent visitor. The Abbey, which purports to have both a secret passage to Great Missenden Abbey and a ghost, is now a private hospital.

Little Kingshill: The origins of the village date back to AD 900 and the founding of a monastery. William I gave a manor and lands to the Earl of Aufrics, hence Affricks Farm, now an Elizabethan farmhouse.

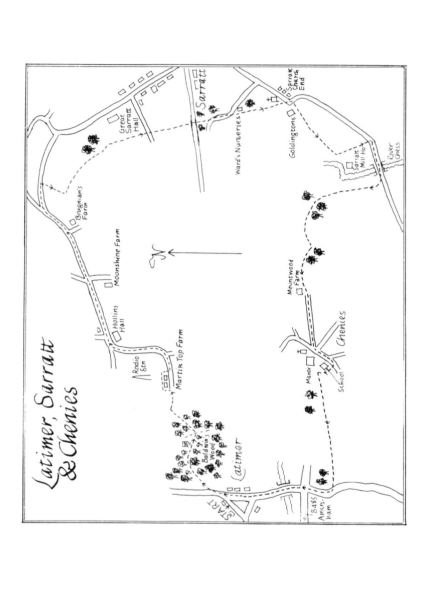

Latimer, Sarratt & Chenies

Latimer

START

Baldwins Wood

Martin Top Farm

Radio Stn

Hollins Hall

Moonshine Farm

Brugman's Farm

Great Sarratt Hall

Sarratt

Ward's Nurseries

Goldingtons

Sarratt Church End

Sarratt Mill Ho

River Chess

Mountwood Farm

Chenies

Manor

School

B485 Ames-ham

Latimer, Sarratt and Chenies

Introduction: This walk passes through the 3 charming villages of Latimer, Sarratt and Chenies. Sarratt is just into Hertfordshire and the other 2 are in Buckinghamshire. Some of the most dramatic of Chiltern scenery is there to be enjoyed while the villages themselves, Chenies high above the Chess valley and Latimer and Sarratt on lower ground, are a pleasure to walk through. The walk starts in Latimer, with a steep climb to Martin Top Farm and a large radio station, then on to Sarratt on level ground and downhill to Church End and Sarratt Bottom, across fields and through woodland to Chenies, with its lovely mellow red brick manor house dating from the 15th century. Recrossing the tiny river Chess, the walk returns uphill to Latimer.

Distance: 7 to 8 miles. A pleasant non-taxing walk with only 1 brief steep uphill climb. It is worth allowing 3½ hours or so, so that the villages can be explored too. OS Map Sheet 166 Luton & Hertford.

Refreshments: There is a pub, the *Cock*, at Sarratt Church End which serves good bar meals and lies almost exactly halfway along the route. There are no other places for refreshment en route but there are many delightful spots in which to picnic overlooking beautiful rolling countryside.

How to get there: From Amersham take the A404 (Watford) road up Stanley Hill and, at the double mini-roundabouts at the top, go straight ahead for 1 mile and then take the signposted left turn for Latimer. After another mile turn right for Latimer and left at the crossroads over the river Chess. Park the car on the left by a white house, on the far side of a small triangular village green.

The Walk: On leaving the car turn left on to the road and after ¼ mile take the marked footpath on the right, climbing uphill toward a wood. Enter the wood and, ignoring the yellow arrow at the top of the path, turn right on to a path. At the top of the path, emerging into more open country again, bear left opposite a fence and go straight ahead along a track which crosses another in a dip. On the right is a small wood in which you can see charcoal burners at work. At the farm yard (Martin Top) turn left and then right twice to go through the farm buildings and get back on the same path. Turn left onto a wide farm track and left again at its end on to a lane. Pause here to absorb the view of the sweeping landscape on the right. The radio station at RAF Chenies lies on the left.

Walk along the lane under high old hedges which form an arch overhead for ¾ mile and then turn right at Hollin's Hall as for Belsize. Follow this lane for about 1½ miles past Moonshine Farm and Bragman's Farm on the right.

At the fork in the road turn right and, after 200 yards, take a path for Church End and Chenies on the right. Turn left to skirt the farm buildings and follow a broad track through open fields and then mixed woodland on the left. Take a marked path on the right approximately 50 yards before a modern house on the left which stands on the road to Sarratt. Follow the path across open fields behind Great Sarratt Hall to a small lane. Cross the lane to a stile. Over the stile follow the path keeping the hedge on the left, across a field with sweeping views of farmland and woods. Next comes a stile and 'squeezer' into another field. Cross to a wood which, so says a plaque on the left, was planned and planted by one, Frederick Ward. Cross a ride and forge straight ahead to another lane and to a path concealed in the hedge in the righthand corner opposite Ward's Nurseries. Bear right at the fork, go through a gate to a track and turn right through another, waymarked gate 20 yards on. Walk straight ahead keeping the woods on the left and open fields on the right, across the common to the pretty church of the Holy Cross at Sarratt Church End. Walk through the churchyard; notice the memorial on the left by the church. A small girl stands on tiptoe to hang a wreath around the head of a cross. The lettering below is mostly unreadable.

Outside the churchyard, turn right and then left onto a marked footpath. Keeping the fence and a grand house, Goldington's, on the right, go straight ahead downhill with views of the deep Chess valley below. Go over a stile and turn left onto a track which emerges onto a road, where turn right. Cross the river by a small bridge; Sarratt Mill, now a dwelling house, lies on the right. Turn right after the river crossing onto a marked path for Sarratt Bottom and Chenies and, after 1 mile, take a left fork away from the river and turn left over a stile and go uphill into the wood. Take the path on the right out of the wood into a big field, bearing left at the field edge with the hedge on the right. Turn right at a grass triangle at the hedge end along the side of the wood on the left. Turn half left through a metal gate on to a farm track and follow this to Chenies. The church and Chenies Manor lie up a gravelled drive opposite. The Manor is open to the public most days and is well worth a visit.

Cross the road over a triangle of grass opposite the drive to the Manor and turn left up the lane for about 100 yards. Just past the school on the right, take the marked bridleway on the right. In 50 yards climb over a metal gate and in another 50 yards turn right again past the back of Chenies Manor on the right and Chenies Farm on the left. Ahead you will see a white sign with 'Car Park' in bold red lettering on an outbuilding. Turn left here and go through a gate onto a track through woods.

Follow the track along the contour of the hill. There are glimpses of the river Chess sparkling through the trees, Latimer House lies up the hill ahead with some splendid views over the valley and Latimer village lies in the hollow below on the right. Soon the track runs through woodland again and there are many Spanish chestnut trees, the prickly husks of the the fruit scrunching underfoot as one walks. The track emerges onto a lane. Turn right downhill toward Latimer, crossing the busy valley road with care, and over the river by a pretty little bridge and so uphill to Latimer and the car.

Historical Notes

Latimer has existed since Roman times; the first mention of the manor being later in 1194. Latimer is named after the family to whom Edward III granted the manor. Both Charles I and Charles II are said to have stayed there. The present house, amid rolling parkland, was rebuilt in 1863 as a large Tudor-style mansion of red brick with stone dressing. Near it lies the rather unremarkable Victorianised church of St Mary Magdalen. On the little triangle of village green is a memorial to a horse, wounded during the Boer War, captured and brought to England by Major General Lord Chesham KCB. There is also a tiled pump which was used by the villagers as their water supply until 50 years ago when mains water was brought to the village.

Chenies lies on a hill above the valley of the Chess; it takes its name from the Cheyney family who were lords of the manor. In 1526 John Russell married into the family. Henry VII made him a Gentleman Usher at court, under Henry VIII he became Lord High Admiral of England and served both Edward VI and Mary Tudor as Lord Privy Seal, subsequently becoming the first Duke of Bedford.

A younger son of the sixth Duke, Wriothesley Russell, became the rector of Chenies in 1829 at the age of 25 and remained there until his death in 1886, declining offers of higher church office. He taught the local children to read and write in classes held in the rectory kitchen.

In 1954 the Duke of Bedford sold his Chenies estate, but it is still in the Bedford chapel of St Michael's church, built in 1556, in Chenies that the Dukes of Bedford are buried.

The present manor is of 15th-16th century origin, L-shaped and built of dark red brick with steep gables and ornamented brick chimneys. Built a little to the east of the site of the original Chenies Manor, it contains portraits of the Russell family and many charming family pieces.

Sarratt, on the edge of Hertfordshire, was probably a stopping-place for drovers on their way to London with geese, sheep and other livestock. There is a wide village green with 3 ponds on it. There were, at one time, 5 inns surrounding the village green, the oldest of which, *The Boot*, dated 1739 remains. It is thought to be much older than its date.

The Saxon church of the Holy Cross at Sarratt Church End lies outside the main village; at Sarratt Bottom, deep in the Chess valley, there were, at one time, both a flourishing mill and watercress beds.

Aldbury
and Ashridge

Introduction: This short walk is particularly attractive on a fine autumn afternoon when the low sun glances through the woods, of birch, oak and beech, creating deep blue-grey shades in the hollows and highlighting the striking hilltop view of one of the prettiest villages among those nestling in the folds of the Chiltern hills. Superb parkland and the extravagant mansion of the Duke of Bridgewater, famous for his pioneering of canal-building in this country, contribute to the pleasures of the walk. Much of it is through National Trust property, the Ashridge estate, and passes by the Bridgewater Monument, high on the hill above Aldbury.

Distance: 5 miles - easy enough walking and there are no stiles! Allow about 2 hours. OS Map Sheet 165 Aylesbury & Leighton Buzzard.

Refreshments: The *Greyhound* at Aldbury is a welcoming and popular pub and offers a good menu of bar meals.

How to get there: Proceed through Tring towards Watford and leave the town by an unclassified road signposted to Tring station and Aldbury. After about 1½ miles the station is passed on the right and the road narrows into a lane winding uphill to the village of Aldbury. On entering the village pass the church on the left and then turn left by the duck pond to park in the wide centre of the village street.

The Walk: Walk along the left side of the pond and turn left into Toms Hill Road. After about 50 yards take a left fork into a lane leading uphill past the old rectory. Carry straight on up the path, ignoring all side turnings, to the top of the hill. Notice, as you walk up this deeply-sunken lane, how the clawlike roots of the beech trees cling tenaciously to the steep banks of the lane as if fearful of losing their balance! The trees open out toward the top of the hill on the left to give a magnificent prospect of patterned fields and hill contours with the woodland dropping steeply away below. There is a bench on the right where one may sit to admire the view and catch one's breath after the short climb.

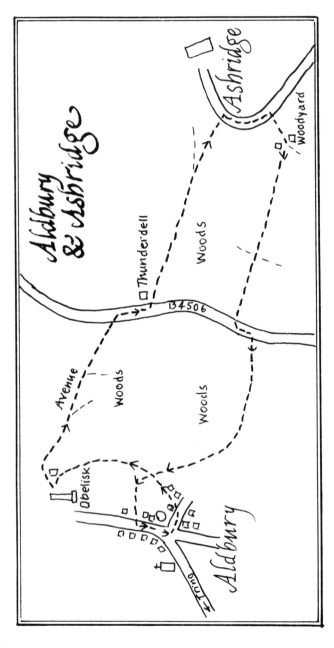

At the top of the hill is the rather austere Bridgewater Monument, a 100 ft high pillar round the top of which is a railed platform. There are some very fine views from the top of the pillar, which is open to visitors during the summer every day but Friday. Bear right here past the Ashridge Visitors' Centre and Shop and then straight ahead along the broad avenue. This lovely avenue is a splendid mix of oak, beech, birch and some Spanish chestnut and the blend of colours in the autumn sunshine is quite spectacular.

Where the avenue emerges on to a road turn right and walk down the road to a white/grey lodge, Thunderdell, and take the path alongside it on the left. This is a metalled track and is used by cars on estate business so it is advisable to keep to the verge. After about ½ mile the metalled track goes off to the left but the path continues straight ahead and it is here that small herds of deer may well be seen grazing among the trees.

At the end of the path turn left up the road to view Ashridge House, a 19th century mansion now housing a Management College. Having seen the house, return past the junction with the path and walk on down the lane for about 400 yards and turn off right down a bridleway marked 'Private Road - Woodyard and Coldharbour' and, where the track turns sharply left, turn right on to a grassy path, ignoring the stile on the right. There is a house set in woods on the left. The serene, tree-studded parkland on the right still shows the signs of devastation caused by the 1987 hurricane.

Keep the fence of the park on the right till it turns right on a corner and here keep straight on, through a wood of Spanish chestnut and oak trees, ignoring side turnings until a road is reached. Turn left on to the road and follow it for about 300 yards and then take a marked bridleway on the right. Keep straight ahead on the bridleway, crossing a broad path across the way signposted 'Marked Walk' and bear a little to the right at the fork in the path after 50 yards. Go straight ahead past a white cottage on the right and across a crossing-path.

At an open ridge with a wonderful view overlooking Aldbury and the surrounding countryside, turn right and walk across the top of the field past a wooden seat and into high woodland again. Cross a path and follow straight on, keeping a wire fence on the left. There are glimpses of well-kept and attractive gardens on the left and the branches of a fallen tree across the path form a perfect O-shape. Cross the original sunken path and go up on to the ridge on the other side, then follow the path sharply downhill to an iron fence at a field corner. Follow the path round the fence; the wooden fence on the right soon gives way to afford a lovely aspect of undulating countryside ahead. The path goes past some pleasant modern houses on the left to emerge on to the road at Aldbury opposite a black and white timber-framed cottage. Turn left on to the road to walk back to the car.

Historical Notes

Aldbury: The church of St John the Baptist is of 13th century origin; its tower is 14th century and a beautiful 15th century stone screen encloses the Pendley Chapel and the tomb of Sir Robert Wittingham and his wife. In the churchyard is a 300 year old sundial on a wooden pedestal.

The stocks beyond the green and duck pond were last used in 1835 and stand in front of the late 16th century half-timbered manor house.

Bridgewater Monument was built in 1832 to commemorate the 3rd Duke of Bridgewater, owner of the Ashridge estate and a pioneering canal-builder. His first canal was the 40 mile long Bridgewater Canal, built to carry coal from the Duke's estate at Worsley to Manchester and later extended to join the Mersey at Runcorn. It was built by James Brindley in 1761.

Ashridge: The site of Ashridge House was a monastery from the 13th century until it was dissolved by Henry VIII, who used the house to accommodate his young children. Edward VI, Mary Tudor and Elizabeth all lived there before coming to the throne. It was rebuilt by the architect, James Wyatt, in 1808 in the form of a battlemented and turreted neo-Gothic mansion. It has a frontage of 1,000 ft flanked by towers and a hall nearly 100 ft high. In 1928 the house was presented to the Conservative Party as a Memorial College to a former Prime Minister, Bonar Law.

The surrounding parkland was laid out by Humphry Repton and Capability Brown. The park today is home to fallow deer, muntjac, badgers, foxes and hares.

WALK SEVENTEEN

Totternhoe and Dunstable Downs

Introduction: This walk encompasses some of the most dramatic of Chiltern scenery. It begins on the plain at Totternhoe, walking the old 'Church End' part of the village and past the 14th century church of St Giles to Doolittle Mill, alongside a tiny tributary of the river Ouse. It then rises steeply uphill to the top of the Downs where most spectacular views of the surrounding countryside may be had. The route back follows a leafy lane across the fields to Totternhoe. A short diversion will take the walker to Totternhoe Castle, a Bronze Age fort and, later, a Norman castle. The earthworks, motte and bailey are still discernible.

Distance: The walk is 6 miles long and the diversion to the castle is another 1 mile. Unfortunately the walk occupies the edges of 2 OS Map Sheets, 165 Aylesbury & Leighton Buzzard and Sheet 166 Luton & Hertford. Allow at least 3 hours as there is a very steep climb in the middle, which affords an opportunity to stop half way and admire the view and get back one's breath for the rest of the ascent.

Refreshments: There is a pleasant picnic area at Totternhoe Knolls Nature Reserve where the car is parked and there are 2 pubs in the village; one on each side of Church Road. The *Old Farm Inn* on the right serves traditional ales and home-made food and the *Old Bell* is on the left. The Information Centre at the top of the Downs has a snack bar which is open during the summer at peak times.

How to get there: From Dunstable (M1-Exit 11) take the B489 for Tring. At a small roundabout on the edge of the town turn right down a suburban road signposted 'Nature Reserve'. After 1½ miles the road forks and here take the right fork into Castle Hill Road. Park the car in the Totternhoe Knolls Nature Reserve on the right in about ½ mile.

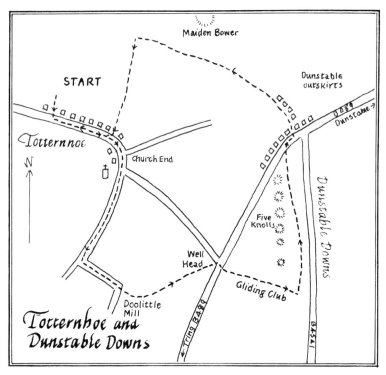

The Walk: Retrace the route down Castle Hill Road and, at the fork, turn right into Church Road. There is a charming mix of old and new architecture here with some delightful thatched and timber-framed cottages; the modern houses blend in quite well. Walk down Church Road. St Giles' church stands back in a clump of trees on the right and, if you are lucky enough to find cleaners or flower-arrangers at work inside, it is well worth joining them for a look at this charming small 14th century church, with patterns of old post mills scratched into the soft surface of the Totternhoe stone from which it is built.

Go on down the road for ½ mile and then turn left into Doolittle Lane where the rather grand Warehill Equestrian Centre lies on the right. Shortly the lane makes a sharp turn to the right and, on the left, is Doolittle Mill, a combined water and wind mill with its tower still visible in the building.

Just before the mill, turn left on to a bridleway and follow this untidy and sometimes muddy track for a little over 1 mile alongside a tiny stream, a small tributary of the river Ousel which joins the larger river

Ouse at Milton Keynes. There are views of comfortable farmland on the left and the wooded banks of the stream on the right. Through a wooden gate the track opens out a little and, on the right, a deep wooded gorge appears. Ahead are dramatic views of the hills, the lion carved into the chalk below Whipsnade Zoo and a glimpse of Ivinghoe Beacon to the far right.

The track leads through a second gate into Well Head Road. Here turn right and, after a few yards, cross the busy B489 to a path opposite leading uphill alongside the headquarters of the London Gliding Club. Soon on the right can be seen the white swiss-roll shapes of the huge transporters used for the gliders. Follow the path keeping the hedge on the right and a steep, scrubby bank on the left, across a field and then through hedges again and out into the open at the foot of the valley.

If you long for a cup of tea at the Information Centre at the top of the hill in front of you, turn right here at a Circular Route marker and follow the path along the valley foot for about 300 yards, then turn left sharply uphill. Pause half way to take in the marvellous view; Edlesborough church perched up on its high mound to the left, Totternhoe and its pattern of farmland ahead and the outskirts of Dunstable to the right. Take the left fork near the top of the hill and then turn right on to the path for the Information Centre.

If tea is not on your agenda, do not turn right at the Circular Route marker but forge ahead on a steep path uphill. At the top of the hill turn left to go along a path parallel with the B4541 Dunstable/Whipsnade road. Follow the path up and down and round a great bowl in the hills formed by the scouring of a deep dry valley and notice the lovely contours and curves of the fields below. On the right there is a glimpse of the great industrial areas of Luton and Dunstable. Soon the path leads downhill to the Five Knolls burial mounds and on, past this ancient monument, downhill to a grassy area.

Cross the grass to the roundabout and go straight across the main (Tring) road here. Turn right and go through a gap in the iron fence on to a track running between the backs of houses. Soon the track goes through another set of iron railings and the houses are left behind and there is pleasant turf underfoot. There are wide views; Ivinghoe Beacon away to the left and the tall chimneys of Pitstone cement works in the far distance ahead. Ignore all side turnings and follow the path as it narrows between high hedges of bramble, buckthorn, hawthorn and dog rose and, in summer, high plants of cow parsley. The path finally opens out again and ahead can be seen the scarred flat surface of a disused chalk quarry. Maiden Bower lies in the field to the right.

Here turn left on to a broad track across the fields, leaving the quarry on the right and follow the well-used path back into Totternhoe village, emerging into a housing estate built round a green. Cross the green and walk down the road straight ahead to the main road opposite a lovely black and white timber-framed house. Turn right here and follow the road back to the car park.

To find the castle, take the footpath on the right at the bottom of the car parking area and follow it, past a large black tank on the left and then a deep leafy hollow with houses at its bottom. Totternhoe Nature Reserve, managed by the Beds & Hunts Wildlife Trust, is all around and the walker is asked to have care for the rare wild flowers, orchids and trefoil in particular. The path forks a little way ahead and there is a notice saying: 'Horses Please Use Other Path'. The walker should take the left fork which emerges, in a few yards, to a flat area of greensward enclosed by a deep motte and bailey. This is all that remains of ancient Totternhoe Castle, high on the hilltop, beautiful and peaceful and with an immense feeling of 'history' about it.

Historical Notes

Five Knolls is the best example of Neolithic/early Bronze Age burial mounds to be found in these hills. Skeletons of Saxon warriors have been excavated from the mounds, indicating that it was a place of burial after a battle. The site was used for a gallows in medieval times.

Maiden Bower was originally a Neolithic site and later became an Iron Age fort. It had 5 entrances and large ring pits, outside the external wall, where the bones of animals, some weapons and pottery have been found and which verify its age.

Doolittle Mill is unusual in combining the use of both wind and water to keep it going. It was shattered by a storm in 1880 and has not been a working mill since. Doolittle was the name often given to the first mill on a stream where the water would not have been very powerful or plentiful.